Praise For *Failu*

Mike Courtney deals with subject matter that is serious and more prevalent than we want to admit. The church must find answers and offer them—because without divine intervention, bondage and hopelessness will prove to be the result. Not only is the individual held captive by addictive practices adversely affected, but every family member is impacted, and the compulsive practices often spread like a contagious disease. We have so much to learn in order to offer help, and Mike's true-life story provides both inspiration and direction. I'm so thankful the story has been shared.

JAMES ROBISON
President and Founder
LIFE Outreach International

I have known Mike Courtney my entire life. Literally. He was there the day I was born--at least I think he was. I heard that he was there. His healing journey has been an inspiration to countless others who found themselves masking pain with a variety of addictive behaviors. Now joy has replaced the mourning, beauty has taken the place of ashes. Secrets have faded away and addiction is stripped away without the fuel to thrive.

Chonda Pierce
Author, Comedian

Mike Courtney has provided a resource for all of us by telling his own story in *Failure and How I Achieved It: A Journey from Addiction to Hope.* This book would be particularly helpful for Christians who are experiencing a "Jekyll and Hyde" life and want to experience a conversion in their own lives which can lead to healing from an addiction to lust. This book can also be a helpful manual for counselors who work with the many Christians who are addicted to lust.

Dr. Ralph H. Earle, Ph. D.
Director, Psychological Counseling Services

In his book, *Failure and How I Achieved It*, Mike Courtney masterfully draws us into the world of addiction so realistically that we can almost feel the struggle with him. Not only does he explain historical events feeding the development of his "disease to please", he takes us through the painful paths of therapeutic interventions and shows us the amazing power of God's love and grace.

I believe this book will be helpful to many—not just those struggling with personality issues. I intend to recommend it to any and all of my clients who are fighting addictions, but also self-esteem concerns, control issues, and family dysfunction. And for those who have trouble believing God loves them, there is hope here.

Alison Y. Evans, Psy. D.
Chair, South Carolina Mental Health Commission

Failure And How

I Achieved It

a journey from addiction to hope

Mike Courtney

ISBN 10: 0-9788304-0-7

ISBN 13: 978-0-9788304-0-3

Printed in the United States of America

The 12 Suggested Steps
of Alcoholics Anonymous

1. We admitted we were powerless over alcohol--that our lives had become unmanageable.
2. Came to believe that a Power greater than ourselves could restore us to sanity.
3. Made a decision to turn our will and our lives over to the care of God as we understood Him.
4. Made a searching and fearless moral inventory of ourselves.
5. Admitted to God, to ourselves and to another human being the exact nature of our wrongs.
6. Were entirely ready to have God remove all these defects of character.
7. Humbly asked Him to remove our shortcomings.
8. Made a list of all persons we had harmed, and became willing to make amends to them all.
9. Made direct amends to such people wherever possible, except when to do so would injure them or others.
10. Continued to take personal inventory and when we were wrong promptly admitted it.

11. Sought through prayer and meditation to improve our
    conscious contact with God, as we understood Him,
    praying only for knowledge of His will for us and the
    power to carry that out.
12. Having had a spiritual awakening as the result of
    these steps, we tried to carry this message to alco-
    holics, and to practice these principles in all our
    affairs.

The Twelve Steps are reprinted and adapted and a brief excerpt
from the book, *Alcoholics Anonymous* is reprinted with permission
of Alcoholics Anonymous World Services, Inc. (AAWS) Permission
to reprint a brief except from the book, *Alcoholics Anonymous* the
Twelve Steps does not mean that AAWS has reviewed or approved
the contents of this publication, or that AAWS necessarily agrees
with the views expressed herein. A.A. is a program of recovery
from alcoholism only – use of the Twelve Steps in connection
with programs and activities which are patterned after A.A., but
which address other problems, or in any other non-A.A. context,
does not imply otherwise.

Dedication

My family is different from most. For some reason God chose to bless me with a wife and two sons that endured the worst I could dish out and, in spite of their own pain, never gave up on me. If I could withdraw the suffering I caused them, I would. Since I cannot, at least my prayer is that in this book they will get the credit they deserve for being beacons of the goodness of God in the midst of the darkest of storms. I also pray that they will see how God has, and will, use them for His Glory.

To Doris

You are the nearest human example of the love, grace and mercy of Christ I will ever be privileged to know this side of Heaven. You still light up my life.

And to Joshua and Jacob

You are my hope and my joy. God used you to draw me to the light and He will use you in greater ways to do the same for others.

"The Lord said, 'I have loved you with an everlasting love. With unfailing love I have drawn you to myself. I will rebuild you. You will again be happy and dance merrily with tambourines.'"
Jeremiah 31:3-4

Acknowledgements

Thank you just doesn't do it. I literally would not be alive today were it not for family and friends that invested in me when I was a lost cause. Too many people to name have had a part in the miracle of grace that Jesus Christ has extended to me. Here are the most obvious.

My sister, Chonda, has been my strongest encourager and motivator in this journey and in this writing project. I go on because of her.

My brother-in-law and my friend, David, has shared generously his expertise in writing and his gift of story. Without his advice, this book would not be.

My beautiful daughter-in-law, Jennifer, an English teacher, has corrected my many grammatical mistakes and been my greatest fan.

Barbie and Dee White, family counselors in Nashville, Tennessee recognized and communicated both the good and the bad in me and pointed me to a place to get help.

Dr. Ralph Earle and the staff at Psychological Counseling Services in Scottsdale, Arizona rescued me from the brink of destruction and facilitated healing.

Our friends, Ravi and Jharna Richards, are the finest examples of genuine Christianity I know, and are teaching me still the joy of being wholly devoted to our Heavenly Father.

My Lord and Savior, Jesus Christ put every one of these people in my path and, when I was at the end of myself, gave me Himself and HOPE.

Finally, the hundreds of people that have loved me when I was unlovely, prayed for me when I did not know it, and helped me when I did not want it, deserve my deepest expression of praise and gratitude.

"May the Grace of our Lord Jesus Christ, be with you all." Galatians 6:18

Step Eight

"We made a list of all persons we had harmed and became willing to make amends to them all."

There is a danger that some would see this book and say, "Well, that is over and all is right with the world." Not so. In my addictive lifestyle, in my sin, I harmed people that, frankly, will carry scars forever. God forgives me, and them. Grace and mercy are offered and the hope of a wondrous life in Him is available, but the fact remains, I hurt people. And for that I am deeply and continually sorry.

Three great churches were set back and robbed of what "might have been" by my actions. I pray for those churches daily and believe that God has great plans for them. But I still mourn the damage that I did and offer my sincere apology.

A number of families were gravely wounded by my actions. I know that God is able, and hopefully has, taken them well beyond the hurt that I caused. I desire the very best for them and am so sorry for the betrayal I committed against them.

Step Nine says, "We made direct amends to such people wherever possible, except where to do so would injure them or others."

To do more than this written apology is not possible. To attempt more would be more destructive than productive. So, I leave the people and the places that I have offended in the hands of God. And I make every effort, from this point on, to do penance by impacting for good, everyone I come in contact with.

"Having had a spiritual awakening as the result of these steps, we tried to carry this message to others and to practice these principles in all our affairs." **Step Twelve**

Foreword

In his book, *Failure and How I Achieved It*, Mike Courtney masterfully draws us into the world of addiction so realistically that we can almost feel the struggle with him. Not only does he explain historical events feeding the development of his "disease to please", he takes us through the painful paths of therapeutic interventions and shows us the amazing power of God's love and grace.

This work is particularly pleasing to me as a Christian clinician, because it points out how beautifully the worlds of psychology and spirituality truly fit together. His explanation of "helping and healing" reminds us that God can do all things—if we allow it. It also puts responsibility on each of us to invest in the journey. We should not just haphazardly wait on God to do it all. He expects us to meet Him in the process.

I believe this book will be helpful to many—not just those struggling with sexual issues. I intend to recommend it to any and all of my clients who are fighting addictions, but also self-esteem concerns, control issues, and family dysfunction. And for those who have trouble believing God loves them, there is hope here.

Thank you, Mike Courtney, for allowing us to learn from your walk.

—Alison Y. Evans, Psy.D
Licensed Professional Counselor
Chair, South Carolina Mental Health Commission

Foreword from Chonda

I have known Mike Courtney my entire life. Literally. He was there the day I was born--at least I think he was. I heard that he was there. I also heard that he carried me to school one day for show and tell. Most fourth grade boys were taking frogs and crickets in jars. My brother took me. Wrapped tightly in a blanket, he patiently and kindly described his treasure to the class while slowly peeling away the covers to reveal my *feet*. He was holding me upside down the entire time! We have joked in our family that that must have been the moment--with blood rushing to my brain and I was moved to become a stand-up comedian.

My professional life has yielded seven books, three CDs and a wall of gold-certified videos. My job description was to evoke laughter from whoever listens but most nights the laughter was merely the catalyst for revealing a much deeper story. My "tell-all" approach was not always embraced much less appreciated by my brother! We have always joked that he's just mad because I told-all first and got paid for it! If that's true – then I owe him!

But the real debt would go back to the day he carried me into the 4th grade for show and tell. You see, my brother took it upon himself to "carry" me and every other burden a childhood of pain, rejection and humiliation has produced. While I told all – he hid all. I think the burdens, the secrets, the rejection finally caught up with him. I'm not surprised – I've been praying for years that it would!

His healing journey has been an inspiration to countless others who find themselves masking pain with a variety of addictive behaviors. For a brief time, I was able to return the huge favor and "carry" him for awhile. That's what you do when someone you love is suffering – you feel like you're carrying the burden with them and for them. But that's okay – he ain't heavy -- he's my brother! I am proud that he is.

Now joy has replaced the mourning, beauty has taken the place of ashes. Secrets have faded away and addiction is stripped away without the fuel to thrive. And me? I have had the best vantage point to watch the burdens disappear into weightlessness. I had an birds eye view. We have both found our wings and learned to fly!

> —Chonda Pierce
> Little Sister

CONTENTS

A NOTE ABOUT THE STORY

There are some heroes in this story. I am not one of them. My incredible wife learned to trust God and endured unimaginable pain, always believing that God would ultimately win out, she is a hero. My two sons became men before their time and yet maintained tender hearts that allowed them to get in touch with the love of Jesus, offering undeserved forgiveness to me, they are heroes. My sister and brother-in-law who came to the rescue of my family, and me, time and time again are heroes. Pastor Jeff is a hero. He walked beside me without judging but also without condoning. There are friends and church leaders, too many to name, who are heroes. They offered love where they could and helped when they were allowed.

The greatest hero of all is a loving, grace-full God. He never gave up, never gave in, never quit tugging and pursuing me. God is the ultimate hero because all of the love and forgiveness and understanding and help that came from everyone else originated with Him. He allowed hurt in order to heal. He allowed failing in order to forgive. He allowed sin in order to save. All He ever asked of me was that I believe that He loved me. And when I finally turned to Him, it was not because I was a hero but because He was. As Augustine said, "If we but turn to God, that itself is a gift from God."

I am not the hero in this story and any hint to the contrary in these pages is a gross mistake. I am a liar, a thief and a cheat. But I am redeemed by a hero. Because of that, it is important for me now to tell the truth, to always tell the truth.

This story is true. But it is my story. In order to protect innocent, and not so innocent people, I have changed the names of people, (except my family), and the names of places. I have also combined stories for the sake of brevity and anonymity, taking an anecdote from one place and inserting it in another. That is to say, the story is true but it is not an historical account, it is a journey, an experience. It is the tale of a hero who uses other heroes to save the most miserable of villains, and to bring them all to a happy ending. And that's the truth.

Chapter 1

PERCEPTIONS

The waiting room of the clinic is unimpressive. A half-dozen, brown, padded, chairs line the walls of the L-shaped room, separated by cheap, dusty fake ferns. The receptionist sits behind a stained formica counter in a cubicle surrounded by tall, gray, filing cabinets.

I usually sit in the same spot, if it is available, a corner chair that has a view of the receptionist at one end of the "L," and the flat oak door at the other. Behind this door are the offices and cubicles we use for the counseling sessions. By the end of the second week, I have browsed through every outdated magazine scattered on the two or three coffee tables. Now I just sit and make notes in my journal as I wait for my next appointment.

It has been a grueling two weeks to say the least. Counseling sessions or group therapy begin at seven AM every morning, Monday through Saturday, and last until nine-thirty or ten PM each night. There is a ninety-minute break in the middle of the day, but since I walk a couple of miles from the cheap hotel to the clinic, I don't have time to go back and rest. Lunch is a box meal that is eaten during group. By the end of everyday, I am mentally and emotionally spent, and by the end of the week, there is nothing left. Physical fatigue and mental exhaustion are constant companions.

As I sit and wait on this day, one of the "inmates," a pock-faced, old man named Frank, sits down beside me. We have learned quite a few things about each other in group but last name is not one of them. I know how old he is. I know where he comes from. I know what he did for a living, and, I know about his offenses, who he touched, and the addiction that brought him to this place. He knows my name is Mike, little else.

He is a nasty man, not the kind of person I would have spent time with on the outside. He has the appearance of an offender. Years of addiction and secrecy have left him furtive looking. He seems to look over me, or behind me, as we talk. His hands never stop moving, picking invisible lent from his wrinkled slacks, or searching his breast pocket for a pen that isn't there. His teeth are yellowed and his skin is scaly. He sits too close and talks too loud, but he has a message that he seems to think I should hear.

"I was praying today and God gave me a verse for you," he says. To my surprise, he pulls out a faded, old, Bible that is well used and heavily marked. "Zephaniah 3:17," Frank blurts, "'The Lord your God is with you, He is mighty to save. He will take great delight in you, He will quiet you with His love, **He will rejoice over you with singing**.'"

And then Frank whispers. Tears are pouring from my eyes so that the waiting room takes on an almost heavenly shimmer and Frank looks like, well, like an angel. He leans even closer and he whispers like a little kid who has discovered what he is getting for Christmas, "Can you believe, the God who created the universe knelt down beside your bed this morning and sang over you?"

"I was born a poor black child." So Steve Martin, the lily-white comedian begins his homily in the 1980's movie, The Jerk. While the movie may not have any other redeeming social qualities, this idea is crucial: *the perception we have of ourselves on the inside is often far different from what others see of us on the outside.* And, it is at this point that much of the internal turmoil and trepidation with which we live, is born.

In "The Problem," a short essay from one Twelve-Step group, it says, "Many of us felt inadequate, unworthy, alone, and afraid. Our insides never matched what we saw on the outsides of others." (*SA Literature*)

The book of James says, "Anyone who listens to the word but does not do it is like a man who looks at his face in a mirror and, after seeing himself goes away and immediately forgets what he looks like." (James 1:23-24)

For some, the gap between internal perception and external reality, or vice versa, is hardly dramatic. Our misconstrued self-portrait may be simply an extra healthy, although misplaced, sense of competence. We were attending a church in Ohio a few years ago and on a Sunday morning one of the teenagers tried to sing the special. She was a Dolly Parton-wanna' be and obviously, like her idol, believed herself to be musically gifted far beyond anything her listeners could hear or imagine. My youngest son, Jacob, who was about four at the time, was sitting on the front pew and at one particularly grating point in the song, stood up in the pew, turned to the congregation, threw his hands up in despair and cried, "This is AWFUL."

The enthusiasm and optimism of youth misled most of us in our younger days to believe we were "ten feet tall and bullet proof." We were all candidates for "American Idol" and participants on Trump's "Apprentice." But then the pendulum swings the other way and we are in the cast of "The Biggest Loser." Much of what adolescence is about is the raging battle between thinking we can conquer the world and being sure we are the ugliest kid in World Civ class. As we mature, hopefully, a more balanced self-image takes shape.

For many, though, the scars and wounds of our early life tipped the scales away from the super image to the other end of the spectrum, and that self-perception stays with us. Childhood abuse, early trauma, teenage failure (real or imagined) and we brand ourselves as unacceptable creatures. The picture we have of ourselves is so contradictory to the way we really are, that we are consumed with shame and guilt over our shortcomings, real or imagined, or we are devastated by feelings of worthlessness and unlovability. When that is the case, the pain of our perception can become out of control and unmanageable. In that situation, we WILL find a way to medicate that pain at all cost.

The methods of medication are as diverse (and sometimes perverse) as the creativity of man. We pop pills, guzzle booze, over spend, over eat, over work. We get high, get laid, get thin, get lost. We lie. We steal. We rage. We despair. Anything that takes our mind off of the hideous face we think we see in the mirror becomes as necessary to life as the air we breathe. Sometimes even a hobby or an interest becomes obsessive. Season tickets to the local sports team, a membership at the country club, even a compulsive need to see our children excel, while not bad in and of itself, can become an insane method of escape from this perceived reality. We may call it a habit, a security blanket, a vice, an obsessive behavior. Whatever we call it, we can't live without it. We are hooked…

WELCOME TO ADDICTION!

Addiction and addictive behavior can be as dramatic and destructive as the junkie we see in the cop show on TV, or it can be as manageable and acceptable as an obsession with reality shows or sporting events. I have known men who escaped from the image they had of themselves by collecting guns or knives to the point of absurdity. I have seen women who spend every waking moment entering their infant daughters in beauty contests and modeling classes. One professional golfer recently admitted publicly to losing over fifty million dollars gambling and said, "If I don't get this under control it could become a problem." We may see our actions to be a quirky personal interest or we may be captive to an addiction that we use to mask the pain of our false self image.

My drug of choice was sex. To be more specific it was lust and the desire to be lusted after. I masked the pain of the false concep-tion of who I was by planning, dreaming about, preparing for, and being involved in lustful relationships. If I could convince myself that there was someone who found me so attractive that she "needed" me then I could forget, for a moment, how undesirable I really was.

But inevitably, the regret, shame, and guilt of that lustful relationship would sweep over me like a hurricane. One affair after another, rather than medicating the pain, only widened the divide between who I thought I was and who I thought I was supposed to be. Instead of covering the pain, my shameful behavior made it deeper. And, as is characteristic of an addiction, instead of stopping, I only craved more of the drug, playing out the whole, sick, cycle again.

I doubt if most psychologists would state that addiction is entirely an acquired behavior. There is a genetic predisposition. There are personal choices. There are the twists and turns of fate, and somehow, even the providence of God. But it was on the training ground of the home where I conceived the coping mechanism that gave birth to addiction. In my home that coping mechanism was secrecy. Just don't talk about it. Refuse to admit there is a problem. And above all never let the world around you know that anything is wrong.

I grew up in the church, as my sister says, "second row, piano side." My parents were ministers and for us there were two worlds, home and church. Nothing existed apart from these two, and the first could never be allowed to taint the second. The secrets that we learned to keep at home should not and could not be shared with the church. Implicit in that lesson was the idea that the church, and God, wouldn't love us if they knew our secrets.

When I was about eight, a cousin came with her family to visit us. She was a few years older than I was, maybe ten. One evening we were playing hide-and-seek with some neighborhood kids. The next thing I knew a police car was in front of our home and the adults were talking in small groups and hushed tones. I came to discover years later that a neighbor boy had molested my cousin. But on that night, the cousin's family left and I never saw her again. And we never mentioned it. In retrospect it might have been an opportunity to teach the children about trust, sexual predators, and self-preservation (especially my three younger sisters.) Instead, we were taught the lessons of shame and secrecy. If one of the children brought it up, we were hushed, and told, "We do not talk about such things in a Christian family."

I preached my first sermon when I was thirteen. My father suffered what we would have called then a nervous breakdown, if we had called it anything. I remember a Saturday night when the shades were drawn, the parsonage (right next door to the church) was oppressive. My mother was crying. My father locked himself in the bedroom with a shotgun and threatened all night to take his own life. On Sunday morning my mother said to me, an adolescent with pimply skin and greasy hair, "You go next door and preach and tell them daddy is sick. Don't let anyone in the church know what is wrong."

I preached on Moses, challenging the children of Israel by asking, "Who is on the Lord's side?" All the while, as a frightened teenager, I was wondering if any moment the sermon would be interrupted by shotgun blast or a scream. It might have been a good time to learn about corporate prayer, divine healing, and the benefit of professional therapy. Instead I learned about maintaining public perception and protecting private secrets.

My parents divorced when I was in college. By then the tumor of deception and dysfunction had become such a huge malignancy that it was impossible to hide. They had tried counseling for years, on and off, and made a number of moves to escape our secrets. My father was still a pastor. He agreed to marry my fiancé and me, in spite of the struggles that I knew my parents were going through. On the day of the wedding, he pulled me aside and said, "After the wedding I'm leaving. My bags are in the car." I didn't tell my mother. I didn't tell my wife until we were on our way to our honeymoon. I had learned to keep secrets.

Doris and I stood in front of an altar and promised to "love, honor, and cherish" while my father was planning to quit and run. We were almost to our honeymoon suite in Gatlinburg when I told her the truth. We left early to go back and take care of my mother and sisters. We never told anyone else. In fact, we really never talked about it much ourselves. Doris did not tell me how she felt about interrupting our honeymoon to rescue my family. I did not ask. Secrets.

Somewhere in the midst of learning to keep secrets and protecting the public perception of perfection I learned a deeper lesson, I was unlovable. The dysfunction and chaos of the home left little time for my parents to be parents. I played baseball, basketball and wrestled from the time I was in junior high school. During that time my parents never attended a single game or came to a single awards banquet. Like most children, I saw myself as the center of my universe. Everything that happened was either, because of me, or about me. In my youthful mind, the reason they did not come was my fault. I understood that the purpose of the secrets they kept was to hide the hideous face I saw in the mirror. Their secrets, and mine, kept people from knowing the real, awful me, because if they knew me, they could not possibly love me.

Dr. Ralph Earle is a nationally recognized expert in sexual addiction and the director of Psychological Counseling Services in Scottsdale, Arizona. He has written several books addressing the childhood roots of the addictive personality. In Lonely All The Time, he writes, "Addicts do not let other people get close to them, because they believe they know exactly what will happen if they do. Experience has taught them that anyone who gets close will almost always hurt them or abandon them. Virtually all sex addicts share this belief and it almost always springs from their rocky childhoods." (Lonely All The Time, pg. 78)

Every teen who has ever popped a pimple or zapped a zit, knows what it is like to feel unlovable. I have to be cool to be in. I have to stay funny to have friends. I have to dress right, drive right, walk right, and talk right to be liked. Nike has made billions, not selling tennis shoes, but selling image. I-pods don't deliver downloads, they deliver hip. I think the Bible says, "Where two or three are gathered together, one of them is going to be left out." We all go through that period of feeling awkward, awful and out of place. We have to do something, or be something, in order to be loved.

Class clown, rebellious daredevil, even straight A, teachers pet, are often attempts to be loved and accepted.

But the lesson of *unlovability* (I made that word up), when reinforced by rejection and loss, can become an obsession. My dad left. My sisters died. The church turned its back. God was silent. The desire to be loved became an addiction. My sexual addiction was not about sex. It was about a desperate search to find someone that could tell me what I was convinced was not true, that I was a person of value, of worth: that I was a person that deserved to be loved. And that secret, shameful, search took place while I maintained the façade of loving father, faithful husband, and successful pastor of large, fast growing churches.

Chapter 2

THE CALL

"What do you make up about that?" asks Carl. It is one of his favorite questions. He is my primary therapist at The Clinic. Dr. Rivers, Carl, is not much older than I am. His background is in ministry and his story may be similar to mine. The therapists at The Clinic get close but not too close. By the end of the two weeks I feel like I know them well, but as I stop and reflect, I realize that they have revealed very little of themselves after all.

I think Carl was a pastor at one time. I think that he went through some of the struggles that I went through but I don't know if he told me that or if I just felt it from our conversations. I talk to him more than any of the others. He is responsible for my case file and at the staff meeting at the end of each week he is the one who oversees my evaluation.

There are a dozen or so counselors and therapists at The Clinic. I have not seen them all, maybe six or seven. Some are warm and engaging, personal in their approach. A couple are very clinical, detached, academic, more surgeon than family doctor. I meet with a counselor several times a day in one on one sessions and then in group three or four times.

But Carl is who I see most often. Every day, sometimes twice a day, we sit in his small office, he in a stuffed desk chair with three wheels and two arms, and me on the end of a cracked, tan, leather sofa with faded plaid pillows of beige, red and hunter green. Today he is asking me about the church and my place in it.

"Why is the church such a comfortable place for your addiction?" he asks again. "Would you have faced the same issues if you were an attorney, or a banker or worked on an assembly line?"

"I don't know," I reply. "I don't know if I would have had the same problems but I do know it wouldn't have cost me as much. I could have been a banker and had an affair and nobody would have cared or even known." I look at his face to judge his response. Sometimes I think I know what he is getting at, I think I know what he wants me to say, but I don't know if that is what I really feel. Even in this place, honesty is a problem for me. I am more interested in pleasing this psychologist and making him feel good about his work than in telling the truth so that I can get well. I have spent a lot of years on the other side of the therapy session. I asked the questions. I helped the patient make the applications. The client came into my bookshelf lined office and sat on my overstuffed, leather chair. I directed the process. Now I feel out of control to have the tables turned.

"I have often wondered if I was genuinely called into the ministry or if I was driven there by the demons in my life," I continue, "I mean did I become a pastor to help people or to meet a need in my own twisted brain? I'm not sure anymore."

Carl has a favorite question that he asks often. He asks it again. "And what do you make up about that?" he queries. "Tell me about your start as a pastor."

I was called to preach in Goose Creek, South Carolina. (There really is a Goose Creek.) It was the summer after my senior year of high school and I was traveling with a church youth group in an old blue bus. We moved from city to city, staying in people's homes or sleeping on the floor of the little churches that we visited. During the day we would knock on doors in the surrounding neighborhood and invite folks to church. At night we would perform a musical (or not so musical) concert complete with drums, guitars, accordion and fifteen fairly off-key teenagers. When the concert was over, our director would preach a brief message and give an invitation to come to the altar. Every night the altar would be filled usually with the same fifteen fairly off-key teenagers. But it was ministry and it was fun.

I grew up in a parsonage but never really thought much about a future in the church. In fact, I never really thought much about a future. Life pretty much consisted of skipping geometry, trying to find a date for Friday, and ignoring the latest crisis at home. The future for a seventeen year old, at least for me, was no further than next Thursday at two PM.

During the choir tour though, I began to think about things. On one of those nightly trips to the altar God really did speak to my life in a personal way. I remember a clear awareness of forgiveness for all of the wicked and horrible atrocities I had committed in my seventeen years. And I remember something else, a desire to do something spectacular for God. Not just some plain old, ordinary, run of the mill ministry. I wanted to change the world for Jesus.

I had been "preaching" quite a bit since that first sermon at thirteen, at least enough to learn that I was pretty good at it. Public speaking and the gift of gab was natural for me. When you are a teenage preacher you don't really have to say much to be cute. Just being on the platform is novel enough to attract people and to win their approval. There was another valuable lesson, preaching gets me strokes. When I was finished people lined up to tell me how good I was and how much they liked me. (Note to self: preaching might be a way to be loved.) In ministry I had discovered something that would earn me the love of God and hide the awful person I was from everybody around me, even fool them into liking me. Two not so profound thoughts were at the center of this revelation, preaching is a good thing. It helps people. And secondly, it is really not that hard. Here was the launching pad for a world changing ministry; it's not bad and I can do it.

So, it was on a Friday night in Goose Creek, South Carolina that I was called to preach. Before the concert we were wandering through the little church, praying and getting psyched for the service. I stopped in an elementary age Sunday School classroom and knelt down in front of one of the pint sized chairs that circled the walls. I prayed for direction, for a word, for anything to make me more deserving of God. When I lifted my head I was looking right at a Bible verse, printed in crayon by some fourth grader. I'm sure it was there before I started praying but I only saw it then as if it were God's handwriting on the wall. "Matthew 28:19-20: Go and make disciples of all nations, baptizing them in the name of the Father and of the Son and of the Holy Spirit, and teaching them to obey everything I have commanded you."

In retrospect, I could have been a missionary, or a teacher, or a lifeguard at a church camp. But on that night, for me, it was a call to preach.

There is a way of being humble, self-effacing and servant-like while at the same time soliciting the accolades and praises of those you "serve." Like the comedian who says, "No, no," to the applause while below the sight of the camera his hands are motioning, "More, more," I learned very early on to respond to compliments by saying, "Praise God. He gets all the glory," which only served to draw more compliments. Whether that was a conscious approach or not, I'm not sure, but I do know that the church was a place where I excelled and people noticed.

More important, preaching was a way to make God notice me, to earn his favor. As I look back I realize that even then my underlying concept was of a God who wouldn't love me unless I did something to prove my merit to Him. And since I was so grossly unlovable by nature, it had better be something stupendous.

Carl puts down his legal pad and sits in silence for a moment. He is very comfortable with silence and I am not. "Does that make the call of God any less real?" he asks me. "I don't think so. Abraham may have responded to the call of God in part to get the promised blessing. Samuel may have been motivated by his mother's vision. David probably wanted to get away from the sheep. Scripture is chocked full of men and women who may have had ulterior motives for answering the call of God on their lives yet, in each case, God used them mightily."

He went on, "I have a sneaking suspicion that God looks for less than perfect people often to do His bidding. A. W. Tozer said, 'Those whom God chooses to bless greatly He must first wound deeply.' The story of Samson the womanizer, the redemption of Rahab the prostitute, the power of Peter, the big mouth fisherman, all these are examples of saints blessed immensely by God after being terribly fallen individuals. Maybe their motivation for ministry was that they were trying to climb back from the fall. I am not sure that these men and women, when they followed God's leading had the purest of reasons. Isn't it possible that somewhere in the back of Paul's mind was the thought of 'making up' for being the persecutor of the church? Couldn't it be so that Isaiah was looking for a way to ease the pain of Uncle Uzziah's death when he said, 'Here am I. Send me?'"

Carl opens a drawer and shuffles through some notes. He pulls out a faded, Xeroxed copy of an outline and hands it to me. "I used to preach a little sermon on the life of King David," he says. "He was selected to be king ahead of all of his brothers though they seemed to have more going for them in terms of wisdom, good looks and personality. I Samuel 16:7 says, 'Man looks on the outward appearance but God looks on the heart.' Samuel goes against the grain and anoints the youngest, smallest, smelliest of Jesse's sons, the shepherd boy. And David kills Goliath, withstands the siege of Saul, and becomes the greatest king in the history of Israel."

I look down and follow along on Carl's outline. I am sure now he was a preacher because there are three points. He reads to me but I imagine him, in another life, behind a pulpit in front of a large congregation. He is preaching away.

"GOD CHOOSES WHO HE USES.

I wouldn't have picked David. Abinidab looked better in the kingly robes. Shammah had a politician's personality. David seems to have been the least qualified but he was chosen by God. I don't know why God chose David. I don't know why he chose me, or you. But I do know that God chooses who he uses.

GOD USES WHO HE CHOOSES.

Did you know that David was the greatest king in the history of the nation of Israel? To this day leaders are still measured against the David yardstick. Even the king before David came up short when compared to David. The people said, 'Saul has killed his thousands and David has killed his ten thousands.' God don't make no junk and when he selects you, be certain he will use you to do great things for him.

AND GOD BLESSES OUR MESSES.

David, with all he had going for him, succumbed to temptation and had an affair and even committed murder. But God still used him and blessed him and said of him, 'He is a man after my own heart.' The call of God is still the call of God even when it is given to cracked vessels with scars and warts and hidden hurts. J. R. Miller wrote, 'Whole, un-bruised, unbroken men are of little use to God.'"

I don't respond. I almost don't know that Carl is finished. I am thinking back to my own call and the motives behind it.

In Goose Creek, South Carolina, the summer after my senior year of high school I felt called into the ministry. I probably answered the call for all of the wrong reasons and certainly with very few gifts but it was still what God wanted me to do and what He wanted for my life. I would have carried my demons and diseases into any career field but in the ministry they were magnified. The secrecy that made healing so nearly impossible was surely increased by living in the parsonage. Preaching for popularity was wrong and was a facet of my compulsive need to be loved. But the truth remains, God knew exactly what He was doing and His plans would not be thwarted even by my addiction. His call on my life was genuine and helped shape everything that followed. That call to ministry was rekindled by a season of suffering that struck my family and defined my life for the next decade.

Carl lets all of that hang there in silence for awhile. He is comfortable with silence. Then he stands and walks to the door. I realize that is his signal for, "Times up. Get out." To reinforce that he says, "Let's pick up tomorrow with a discussion of your family history."

Chapter 3

FAMILY HISTORY

Dr. Carl Rivers is the counselor responsible for compiling the long case history in my file. My appointment with him is at the same time everyday, two PM, just after the midday break. He works with a yellow legal pad in his lap and a cheap, ball point pen that he absent mindedly chews on from time to time.

He is a semi-fit man who has the look of someone who used to workout a lot but now walks and plays golf to stay in shape. His hair is the Arizona version of bleached blonde but is generously sprinkled with the gray that his fifty plus years have earned him. He smiles easily and makes me feel comfortable, talking first about football or fishing or the real estate market in Phoenix. He is a nice looking man with a pleasant personality.

Carl has a therapy style that is conversational at best and kind of "interviewy" at its weaker moments. He will make a comment or two and then ask for my response. I am sometimes lulled into feeling like we are two colleagues discussing some psychological nuance until he reaches for the legal pad. When he talks, the pad lays lifeless on his lap. When I talk the pad comes into play and he looks like he is trying to write down every word that comes out of my mouth, not the way an eager college kid would, taking notes in a lecture, but like a reporter recording as many of the facts as possible. He chronicles the development of my addiction, writing down every sordid detail. If I try to gloss over an area he is quick to probe deeper. It doesn't take many days for me to see the pattern, brief, casual conversation that always comes back around to where we left off yesterday. From some of my earliest recollections until what happened last week, he draws from me my story and writes it down, usually without commentary, from beginning to end. The therapy process has taken on a life of its own during these weeks. I have had a little training and done enough counseling in twenty-five years of ministry that I recognize the techniques they employ to make me talk. Some days it becomes a game. Each therapist employs a different tactic, cajoling, badgering or empathizing and I try to guess the attack *du jour*. At times I childishly resist opening up, making them work for the tidbits of information I dole out. On other days my compulsion to please takes over and I gush inner feelings and secret thoughts, not so much to make me whole but to make the counselor happy. How strange that even here I would work harder to impress the other person than to get at the heart of my own issues?

My desire to meet the needs of the other person has been all consuming. I am a dyed in the wool, all or nothing people pleaser. I live by the rule of musts. I must make them like me. I must keep them happy. I must do what they want. I must meet their needs. Harriet Braiker, a well-written psychologist who deals with personality disorders, calls it "the disease to please." It is a compulsion to find my self-worth in the response the other person has toward me.

Parents that were less than present, an unstable adolescence in a dozen new cities, the abandonment by death of people I loved, whatever the causes I am eaten up with a compulsive need to make others love me by making them happy. It is a never ending, un-winnable, resource draining war and I am totally committed to it. My operating system is finely attuned to the mood of the other person and wired to react accordingly.

The disease to please is the most selfish of all diseases. My people-pleasing is never about the other person. It is always about me and what I want and how I feel. It is a pervasive, egocentric, self centered mind set that says, "I am unlovable, so I must make them love me." To do that I exaggerate, bribe, lie and go out of my way to impress. As a child I retold the story of the ballgame to make me the hero. As a pastor, I steered each conversation to a point where I could provide the help, and become the savior. Every encounter is merely an opportunity for me to take care of me. My needs, my desires, my wants and wishes are the dominant themes that are woven into the fabric of each friendship, partnership and relationship. One of the men in my support group now says, "I'm not much but I'm all that I think about." I encourage. I console. I help. I support. And all the while I am trying to make the other person like me enough so that, for just a little while, I can like myself.

Granted, it has had its benefits. I have been seen as a caring pastor, a loving husband, a doting father, a faithful friend. I appear noble and humble and Christlike, seeking to meet the needs of everyone I meet. And it is a sham. What I really am is a selfish, ego maniac who thinks and cares only about getting my own needs met.

The disease to please rears its ugly head in the therapy room. I want to feel good right now more than I want to be well for the rest of my life. I am so stinking selfish that I want the counselor to admire me even if it delays, or even prevents, the healing that I so desperately need. I am here because my life is in shambles and I am an addict and, instead of getting well, I am worrying about the therapist liking me. Go figure.

Maybe Dr. Rivers senses that early on in the session today. This time there is no conversation, no friendly dialogue. He picks up the legal pad, reads the last few lines from the day before, then without expression or judgment asks me just enough to start the story again. "Tell me about you family tragedies," he says as if he were asking what I had for lunch. "Your father left. You lost two sisters. What do you make up about that?" This is my big chance. I will tell him the story of my life and make him feel sorry for me. And like me.

Charlotta was killed when she was twenty. It was Saturday, July 3rd, the day before the Fourth of July. She was on her way to a part-time job in Nashville during an early morning, summer, thunderstorm. The roads were soaked and her orange Maverick began to hydroplane. She spun across two lanes of traffic and the median before sliding into the path of an oncoming car. The driver side door took the impact and she was killed instantly. It was devastating.

I had just resigned from a church in Middle Tennessee where I had been serving as youth pastor. I knew I was away from God and in no position to be in that position. So I quit, took the weekend to skip church and forget about the picture I had of me. I went camping with some friends. We canoed the Buffalo River in Lawrence County, Tennessee. It was an Outdoor Tennessee, postcard weekend. A lazy sun in an endless, blue sky made a canvass upon which was painted the green canopy of shade trees. All of that was reflected in the black sheen of water. We drifted without lifting a paddle from livery to take out point. We laughed. We took pictures. We picnicked. We were in a secret world, separated from the hurt and guilt and fear of the outside by the dark banks of the river and the forgetfulness of youth.

When we got to the take out point, a Tennessee Highway Patrolman was waiting for us. He told me I needed to call home and drove me back to the livery. John Wellman answered the phone at my house. He was my pastor and my boss and a friend of my father's. I was shocked to hear his voice. He got right to the point, "There's been an accident. Your sister has been in a car wreck." I asked the obvious question, "How bad is she hurt?"

Two-word response. The Outdoor Tennessee postcard exploded. "She's dead."

I glance over at Carl. He is writing feverishly. Maybe that is good. Maybe he is really impressed. Maybe he isn't listening at all. Maybe I am wasting his time and mine. The second face of the disease to please is the need to be responsible.

The death of my sister was my fault. Wrath of God, divine retribution, punishment for sin, call it what you like but from that moment on I internalized all of the blame for her tragic, senseless accident and for all of the suffering that followed.

Seventeen months later Doris and I were married and my father left.

His leaving was not really a surprise. He was emotionally absent most of my growing up years. His own demons depleted his emotional reserves so that little was left for parenting. He managed to be an effective pastor in between depressive episodes that sent him into the slough of despond and the family into chaos. At times he found the comfort he craved in external relationships, platonic or otherwise. He had affairs.

I have a great deal of respect for my father and certainly more sympathy than I ever imagined possible. He carried a generational curse that I believe he inherited from his family of origin and that he passed on to me. The tendency to despair, the inability to love or be loved, the hunger for affection and affirmation that no one could fulfill; all were things that were present in him, his family before him and their families before them. In Exodus twenty and verse five (and other places) God promises to visit the sins of the father on the children to the third and fourth generations. I am convinced that the struggles of my father were not generated within his own psyche alone but were passed down to him, at least in part.

Carl interrupts me to agree. He takes a book from his desk as he speaks. "That is not to say that God is such a vengeful God that He spanks children and grandchildren for the deeds of their parents and grandparents. Beth Moore addresses this so well in her book, Breaking Free. She says, 'God does not punish children for their parents' sins......I believe God says He will be able to review or take a census of all the times the effects of parents' sins can be seen in the next several generations.' She goes on to illustrate, 'For instance if a pollster took a census of the number of alcoholics

in three generations of an alcoholic patriarch's family the head count would very likely be high. Why? Because alcoholism was deposited in the family line. It came calling, and an unfortunate number of children and grand children answered the door.'"
(Breaking Free, Beth Moore, p. 92)

On the evening of November 19, the day of my wedding, sometime after seven PM, while the last candelabras were being put away and the rice was being swept from the steps of the church, my father climbed into his little white Datsun and drove out of our lives. I felt that, because I had married, I had given him permission to do that, to leave. The disease to please and the need to be responsible made it clear to me that I should take responsibility for my parents' failed marriage.

Five months later, the world caved in again. Cheralyn was the baby of the family, my youngest sister. Doris and I were just beginning our new life together and my mother was adjusting to life as a single mother. Charlotta had been killed, Chonda was a senior in high school and Cheralyn was a freshman.

She had a part in the high school play, Oklahoma. There were rehearsals all week and the shows on Friday and Saturday. She was elated and it had been a good diversion to keep her mind off of the decimated family. She sang on Friday but on Saturday was too sick to perform. Sunday she was worse. Monday we were at the doctors office and by Wednesday, seeing a specialist. It was Friday evening when the word finally came to us, leukemia.

We had a family ritual when we were growing up. At night, when the last tooth was brushed and the last story told, the four kids would kneel at the living room sofa and pray. I was the oldest, the smartest and the most spiritual so of course my prayers were deeply profound and highly theological. I was ten. Charlotta was next. She loved God and all of the world so her prayers were missional in nature. She prayed for the children in Africa, the families in Afghanistan and the animals in Albania. She prayed a long time. Chonda was the most entertaining. She prayed loud and confessed all of the sins she had committed that day, known and unknown. Many times my parents made notes so they could "discuss" things with her the next day.

Then Cheralyn prayed. Cheralyn prayed one single, simple prayer every night. "Now I lay me down to sleep. I pray the Lord my soul to keep. If I should die before I wake, I pray the Lord my soul to take." It was cute and she was little.

As we grew older our prayers changed. I got even smarter. Charlotta's prayers began to include boys. And Chonda became a little more discreet. But Cheralyn prayed the same prayer. "Now I lay me down to sleep." At times we would have friends over and it would be embarrassing, a junior high school girl praying a kindergarten prayer. I thought she was prayer challenged. I tried to offer suggestions but my mother would say, "Leave her alone. She likes that prayer."

On Friday night in Baptist Hospital the doctor met us in the hall. "Cheralyn has leukemia," he said. She was lying in the room behind us, the door closed unnecessarily because he whispered as he spoke. "It is in the final stages. I would predict less than a month. I'm sorry."

I went back into her room to sit by her bed. The rest of the family scattered to find pay phones and make the appropriate phone calls. It was late by this time and the dark hallway echoed with footsteps when a white shoed nurse would pad by the room. Across the hallway an elderly patient groaned. Somewhere a bedpan clattered and Cheralyn woke up from her fitful sleep. "What's the matter with me Mike?" she asked. I said "Honey, you are really sick." Something in my voice must have relayed more than I intended. "Am I going to die?" she asked.

Cheralyn was fifteen years old, a high school cheerleader, tall, blonde hair, blue eyes. She should have her whole life ahead of her. She should be planning to go to the prom and giggling in study hall. How do you answer that question? "You might, honey," I said. "You just might."

She seemed to think about that for just a minute and then she reached over and patted my hand with a little smile on her face. "That's okay," she said, and she went back to sleep.

A few years after Cheralyn died our first son, Joshua was born. He was a gift from God and I was sure he would grow up to either be the next Michael Jordan or the world's greatest theologian. By day, when he was three, I taught him the behind-the-back dribble and by night, I taught him to pray. I made sure that his prayer was very profound and highly theological. "Now I lay me down to sleep. I pray the Lord my soul to keep. If I should die before I wake I pray the Lord my soul to take."

Carl waits quietly. He seems moved by my story. He picks up the legal pad and looks back over his notes. "You realize now how crazy it is to think that every problem in your family was your fault. I've learned to call that stinking thinking."

I nod, but at the time, that is the place to where my feeble mind fled. Each tragedy in our less than functional family happened because I was so unlovely. And each tragedy reinforced the inner picture that I had of myself as so unlovely. The disease to please came calling often and I always seemed to answer the door. It wasn't a far stretch from the pain of that place to seeking a way to mask the pain with the affectionate response of someone else. The more I hurt the harder I looked. The harder I looked, the more I hurt.

I don't tell Carl these thoughts. If he knew those things about me he might not like me. Better to leave it like it is for today. He tosses the legal pad onto his desk and stands up to open the door. I know we are finished for the day. As I walk out I can't help but question to myself, "I wonder if he likes me."

Chapter 4

AUGUSTA

Andie Bowman is a petite, dark haired woman in her late fifties. She has a professional air about her that is accentuated by the wireless cell phone attached to her left ear. She is attractive, dresses sharp, but the little silver and black cell phone makes her look off balance, like one huge earring is missing. She comes to the waiting room to get me today. I recognize her voice before she opens the door, talking to an invisible other party trapped in that silver and black earpiece.

My sessions with Dr. Bowman are always entertaining. She seems to be the resident expert in off-the wall, out-of-the-box, counseling techniques. She uses drama, candles, games, and music therapy to get to a point in the healing process. Just what that point is, I am never sure, but I am never bored in her sessions. Carl Rivers calls what she does "voodoo." He says no one else at the clinic understands it, but it works.

Apparently he has talked to her about one period in my "story" that he wants to explore further because today she has him come in for the first few minutes of our session. Her office is larger than any of the other offices, (except for the director's, Dr. Dunning) and more nicely decorated. There are two couches, both covered with a bright red, velvet like material, and dozens of pillows. Some of the pillows are thrown haphazardly on the furniture. Some are piled in the corners, black, and red, and blue, overstuffed, well-worn, pillows.

We settle into our places. Dr. Bowman is behind her desk, I am on one of the red couches, and Dr. Rivers is standing by the door. He has the legal pad with him and as we all begin, the two therapists discuss my case as if I am not here. I feel like I am a spectator at my own open-heart surgery. The two surgeons are passing my organs back and forth, commenting on the weight and color, and I am watching the whole thing take place.

"He seems to have had a relatively symptom-free period while they were youth pastors in Georgia," says Dr. Rivers, browsing over his legal pad. "I'd like to go back to that time and examine his marriage."

"We can do that," responds Dr. Bowman. "Look at the size of that kidney. Isn't his liver a funny color?"

We moved to Augusta, Georgia the week after I graduated from college. Everything we owned, Doris and I, was thrown into the smallest U-haul truck available. Doris drove our gold, Chrysler Cordoba, the back seat loaded with our hang-up clothes, and I drove the U-haul. The radio kept me company on the dismal trip from Nashville to Augusta. The most popular song on the airwaves that summer was a country song by Guy Clark that contained the lyrics, "Augusta, Georgia is just no place to be." I heard that a hundred times on the trip down. (A sign from God?)

Doris and I had married a year earlier. She was a dark haired, fair skinned beauty, small, reserved, knock-down gorgeous and completely unaware of it. We met while I was part time youth pastor at her church. She played the piano like no one I'd ever seen and I was instantly smitten. (There's an old word.) I was a too-skinny, greasy haired twenty-two year old, who looked like I was fifteen. I played the trumpet and she was instantly not so smitten. We dated off and on for the two years I was at her church but nothing seemed to come of it.

Six months after Charlotta was killed I called her up. She immediately asked me to marry her, that's the way I remember it, and a year after that we were walking down the aisle of a country church in Ashland City, Tennessee. My family sat on one side in K-mart clothes and with purses full of Prozac. Her family sat on the other side in blue jean coveralls and with hip pockets full of snuff cans. You talk about two worlds colliding, it was a city and country smackdown right there in the pews.

Doris is a testimony to the cliché "Love is blind." If she had seen who she was marrying and what kind of family she was buying into the whole deal would have been off. She might have known though, because when we knelt to pray during the ceremony, my sister, Chonda, had written in white shoe polish on the soles of Doris's heels, "HELP ME!" And God did.

I finished college during the next year while she worked. On weekends we loaded up a sound system in our gold, Chrysler and held revivals in small churches around the southeast. We would be in Aiken, South Carolina one weekend and Dothan, Alabama the next. She played the piano and everybody was amazed and then I preached a little sermon and they all thought I was cute. They liked us. And that felt really good.

And so, when I graduated, we moved to Augusta, Georgia. Doris drove the gold Chrysler and I drove the U-haul truck. I was going to be the youth pastor at a great little church on the east side of town. We were going to do something spectacular for Jesus and make Him proud.

The church was a dark, A-frame building with rust orange pews and communion cup holders in the altar. Two wings ran from each side of the sanctuary lined with non-descript Sunday school classrooms. One wing was the children's classes so all of the furniture was two feet tall, the other was for adults so every classroom was filled with brown, metal, folding chairs. On either side of the platform were two tiny rooms with doors that opened into the choir loft. In the one on the right we kept the choir robes, royal blue, with white sashes, and a heavy, mildew smell. In the little room on the left was my office. I had a desk, two chairs, an old bookcase and a heavy mildew smell. I hung my college diploma on the wall beside a picture of Doris, and one of Jesus because it seemed like the right thing to do, and my "Outstanding Young Men of America" paperweight on the desk.

There were two other buildings on the church property, a free standing fellowship hall because at some point in the past, someone had decided that you couldn't connect a place where you were going to eat with a place where you were going to pray. It was kind of separation between church and plate. The other building was a single-wide, mobile home, a trailer, where the youth pastor lived.

The trailer had been a hot-to-trot swinger's pad at one time, apparently. There was purple, crushed velvet wallpaper on the bedroom walls and mirrors on the ceiling. I kid you not. Doris thought it looked hideous but I said, "Hey, anything for Jesus' sake." There was a living room, so tiny that you could sit on the couch and change the channels on the TV, without a remote, and a kitchen, complete with attached-to-the-wall dining room table. At the other end of the trailer there was a "guest" bedroom and another bathroom, like we planned to have company in 480 square feet. But it was home and we were in love, so we loved it.

The trailer sat right on the two acre asphalt parking lot at the church in Augusta, Georgia. Now you may not know this, but the summers in Augusta are hot. Doris had to keep her make-up in the refrigerator because if she didn't, it would get so hot in the trailer during the day that it would melt. At night it would cool off to ninety-five. Often we would take our blankets and pillows and go sleep on the floor in the fellowship hall. We waited until we were sure no one would be coming by the church, then we would sneak over, whispering and giggling like two kids escaping from summer camp. We would put one blanket on the carpeted floor of the fellowship hall and pull one blanket over top of us. We would go to sleep with Doris' head laying on my shoulder and wake up before anyone came in the morning.

The intense heat in the trailer made all of the wood turn really dry and brittle. The floors would sag and creak when you walked over them. One day I was sitting in the bathroom, you know, sitting. Without warning the floor gave way and I fell through, pot and all to the ground below. Doris was never any help in an emergency. She would start laughing uncontrollably and from then on you were on your own.

Outside our door, on the parking lot was a basketball goal. After church on Wednesday nights the teen guys and I would play pick-up basketball until we were sweaty and stinky. Doris and the teen girls would sit on the steps of the trailer and watch or go inside and eat popcorn. One Christmas I decided to buy a new net for the basketball hoop and, as a joke, I wrapped it up for Doris and put it under the tree. On Christmas morning, when she unwrapped it I could tell she had no idea what it was. In a moment of inspiration I said, "It's sexy lingerie." She wore it three months before she found out different. (Just kidding!)

One night, while we were living in Augusta, someone knocked on the door of the trailer. When I opened the door, a young man was standing on the steps with his hat in his hand and a giant sized grin on his face. He introduced himself as Dewey, a student teacher from Georgia Southern University. He was an All-American golfer and he needed a place to live while he was teaching. We talked for an hour or two and before he left, Dewey had been invited to move in with us. Who knew? The guest bedroom in the tiny trailer would be used after all! He lived with us for six months.

Our days were filled with loving God, chasing teenagers and having the time of our lives. Doris had a job as a secretary in Augusta. I worked in my office planning lessons and writing notes to teens. Every evening we would take the teens to ball games or play volleyball in the church parking lot. We had no money, no time, no privacy and no worries. We were so happy. We fell in love with the little church and they loved us. Any problems or concerns were swallowed up in the enthusiasm of youth. Our faith in God was high and our confidence in ourselves was even higher. Augusta, Georgia was a good place to be.

I haven't noticed that Carl has left the room. Dr. Bowman is laughing and seems to genuinely enjoy the stories of Augusta. That makes me feel good. She pauses for a moment and then puts her counselor hat back on, "There are three stages to a marriage," she says. "There is the honeymoon stage where there is love without knowledge. A couple doesn't really know each other but they love each other and that is enough. Then there is the disillusionment stage where there is knowledge without love. The couple gets to know each other and when they do, they are not sure that they really love each other. Finally there is the intimacy stage, love with knowledge. In this stage the couple really knows each other and they really love each other. Augusta was your honeymoon stage. You were too busy to get to know each other and really didn't know that you didn't know anyway."

Dr. Bowman pauses to turn off the silver and black earpiece that is buzzing on the side of her head. She continues with her instructions. "We are going to do some role playing now," she says. "Based on the things you have told us about Augusta, I want you to act out one of the scenes from your time there. You can use props or pillows or whatever you need. The goal is to relive a moment of joy from those years in Augusta."

I think about that for a minute and then take a folding chair from the corner, "Pretend this is a toilet...."

Chapter 5

MIDLAND

Dr. Carl Rivers is in an unusually good mood today. He is preparing for a seminar that the clinic is putting on for community leaders and I take it from his gregarious demeanor that it means a lot to him. He is leading the seminar and making a presentation in one of the sessions. I sense a chance to get out of confessing so much today so I start asking him about the seminar.

"We've been planning this for a couple of years," he says. "It is a wonderful opportunity to validate what we do here. There are still many therapists who doubt that it is appropriate to use the word addict when referring to a sex or lust issue."

I can tell this is a hot spot for him so I push it a little farther. "How is it an addiction?" I ask. "What are the markers you look for in an addictive personality?"

We are doing more that passing time now. Dr. Rivers is teaching something that matters to him and I am interested in making the personal application. He reaches for a book that he has referred me to a number of times and leafs through some very well worn pages. "Sex or lust is used, in the right person, just like alcohol or drugs. It deadens the senses, masks reality and gives a false sense of power. Addicts, whatever their drug of choice, have some common characteristics," he says, and then begins to read.

"We do know that all addicts have several common attributes, including:

- A tendency to hold low opinions of themselves and to constantly remind themselves of their deficiencies;
- distorted or unrealistic beliefs about themselves, their behavior, other people, and the events that occur in the world around them;
- a desire to escape from or to suppress unpleasant emotions;
- difficulty coping with stress;
- at least one powerful memory of an intense high experienced at a crucial time in their lives and an ever-present desire to recapture that euphoric feeling;
- an uncanny ability to deny that they have a problem."

(*Lonely All The Time*, Dr. Ralph Earle, p.18)

Dr. Rivers catches me by surprise with a question. He turns the tables from being the absent-minded lecturer to being the therapist again. "How do you relate that to your own experience?" he asks. "Does any of that sound familiar?"

I hardly hear the question. I am distracted, thinking about the first characteristic he read, low self-esteem. I especially began to feel that when we moved to Midland.

After a couple of years in Augusta, we moved to Midland, Michigan. The U-Haul truck was a little bigger with a little more cargo and so was Doris. She was expecting Joshua. I called him that through the whole pregnancy, even though we did not know if he was a boy or a girl, until he was born, I mean. When I would call him Joshua, Doris would say, "What are you going to do if this baby is a girl?" To which I would reply, "Call her Joshuette."

The church in Augusta was a nice, little, comfortable place to be. I felt adequate for the task and the old demon of unlovability was mostly silent. Midland was a huge church with a great staff and a long history of excellence. From the first time I walked through the door I was sure that the job was too much for me and I had no business being there. The staff was professional and gifted. They had all been together for a long time and I was the outsider.

Midland is a postcard town. Emerald green fields of corn and wheat begrudgingly make way in the central, Michigan hills for this Norman Rockwell village of two story houses and white-spired churches. When I close my eyes and try to imagine a scene of peace and tranquility, I picture Midland.

The town is built around a park-like square with cobblestone streets and small shops held back by brick sidewalks. Gaslight lampposts mark the corners of each block and every street fades geometrically into neighborhoods. In the center of the square is a civil war statue, surrounded by wrought iron benches and beds of petunias in the spring, and marigolds and begonias in summer and fall. It is, as much as a town can be, heavenly in appearance and attitude. I had my first affair there.

It was winter when the church from Midland invited us up to interview. We flew into Detroit and drove a hundred miles north to Midland. It was evening when we arrived and Doris and I met the pastor, Dr. Gunner and his wife, at a quaint little restaurant on the square, The Alcove. The weather was cold and crisp and, though two Tennessee kids couldn't tell it, the air was ripe with snow. We ate supper and talked about visions and plans and gifts and salary. I told corny, nervous jokes and tried not to spill my 7-UP. Doris was absolutely beautiful in the candlelight of The Alcove. When supper was over and we walked outside onto the square, we were speechless. It had begun to snow while we ate. Snowflakes as big as biscuits were still falling, illuminated by the gaslights on each corner and the streets and sidewalks were blanketed in a perfect, unmarked, fluffy, white comforter of powder. We fell in love with Midland and accepted the job before we ever stepped foot inside the church.

The pastor in Augusta was warm and fuzzy and easy to relate to. The church felt lucky to have us and told us so often. Dr. Gunner was dignified and unapproachable. The church had enjoyed a history of the most gifted leaders in the denomination, and told us so often. My job was to develop a ministry for young married couples, those twenty something and thirty something young professionals that are just starting families and careers and neurotic tendencies. It was a daunting task, several hundred young families were on my responsibility list, but I threw myself into it with all of the zeal that sheer panic affords. The people loved us, the work went well, but I lived with the constant inner terror that someday, someone would find out how inadequate I was.

Every task created more tension, and every success, more pressure. Rather than relieving my anxiety, every time something went well, my performance mentality said, "Great, next time you'll just have to top this." We were surrounded by young people our age, our peers, who apparently liked us and genuinely wanted to be our friends but my insanity saw every overture toward friendship as insincere and held everyone at a distance. My horrible fear was that if they got too close they would see the real me, the me that no one could love.

I realize that there are people who would be shocked to know this. They knew me at that time and believed me to be the most open, compassionate, loving person on the face of the earth. I was accompanied by friends all of the time and everyone felt like I loved them and accepted their love for me. I was always the life of the party. On the outside I was outgoing, fun-loving, and carefree, but the inside of me was frightened, cynical, ashamed and deceitful. One piece of material from a support group that I attend weekly says, "Many of us felt inadequate, unworthy, alone and afraid. Our insides never matched what we saw on the outsides of others." The first time I heard that, it resonated, I understood exactly what it meant.

"And while (we) were there the days were accomplished that she should give birth. And she brought forth a son and wrapped him in swaddling clothes" and laid him in his daddy's arms. Joshua was born in May, our first year at Midland. He was, how can I say it, a perfect child. Maybe it was because of the lack of relationship with my own father, maybe it is because I felt that here was the one person that would really love me, maybe just all fathers feel this way, but I must confess, I was immediately, helplessly, uncontrollably, obsessively in love with my son. I felt, and still feel that way about both of my sons. The one constant, in spite of my addiction and insanity, has always been a passionate commitment to Joshua and Jacob.

Josh was born in the outdated, three story, brick, Benton County Hospital, a block off the square. The year after he was born, they closed the hospital and built a modern complex on the edge of town. The night that Josh was born was the first game of the church softball league. I put on my jersey and cleats just in case and took Doris to the hospital. I figured if the pains were not too close together I could slip away and get in a few innings before I was really needed. Not a good idea. They must have been somewhere between the second and third innings, I was not, when Joshua Jon-Mical came into the world. He was prune-like in both color and texture, slimy and wet, with a J shaped bruise on each side of his face where the doctor used forceps. I thought he was the most gorgeous creature I had ever seen. No matter what else happened, no matter what went wrong, I was certain I would never disappoint this child.

Dr. Rivers interrupts me, "The eighth step of The Twelve Step program for recovery says, 'We made a list of all the persons we had harmed and became willing to make amends to them all.' The darkest side of addiction is that the people we love the most are the ones we hurt most deeply and the most difficult with whom we make amends." He picks up his legal pad and I know I am supposed to continue.

My insecurity about my job was increased by a mounting tension between myself and my boss, Dr. Gunner. My disease to please was especially active where he was concerned. I could teach a lesson and five hundred people would compliment me, but if Dr. Gunner did not commend my work I was defeated. I would finish a project and every leader in the church would acknowledge my hard work and excellence, but if Dr. Gunner did not brag on me, I was demoralized. The pressure that put on our relationship was immense, and all one-sided, but, as I look back, I realize that Dr. Gunner had issues as well that made our work together tenuous at best, and usually, volatile and highly threatening. During one rather heated conversation in my office I asked, probably fishing for a compliment, "Dr. Gunner, do you resent me?" To which he replied, "I have resented you from the first day you started to work here. Before you came I was loved by everyone, now they laugh at your jokes and wait to see you after the service"

I was desperate for affirmation and affection from this senior male (father figure) in my life and, because of his insecurity, he was incapable of showing that to me, at least in my eyes. I felt overwhelmed and under qualified for my job. My wife was busy showering her attention on our new born son. I was a catastrophe looking for a place to happen.

The Bible says in I Peter 5:8 "Watch out for your enemy, the devil. He prowls around like a roaring lion, looking for some victim to devour." The truth is that sometimes he does more prowling than he does roaring. He sneaks up on padded paws and lies in wait, camouflaged in the grass, until the most opportune moment, and then he pounces.

I was unloved and unlovable, at least from my own perspective. No one really knew me and if they did, they would not have liked me. I had no thought of an affair. There was no attraction brewing to the wife of a friend or the neighbor lady next door. I did not burn with lust and I was not tempted by airbrushed pinups or neon lit adult book stores. What I did crave was the escape that would come from someone desiring me as much as I wanted to be desired. Enter the lion.

We had been at Midland for three years and I was overseeing a total restructuring of the church. I was working long hours and trying to visit as many people in this massive congregation as possible in a relatively short period of time. Keeping busy gave me a sense of worth and kept my mind off of my own insecurity. I visited a young adult family, about our age, a couple that we had spent some time with but were not really close to. The Sunday after that visit, Cathy, the young wife, and I were having a conversation in the narthex of the church. She was thanking me for coming by and complimenting me on the job I was doing. As we talked, people milling around us, her tone changed and she started down a path that was unexpected. She began to tell me that her marriage was less than satisfactory. She described a husband who did not respond to her and a life that was not fulfilling. Then Cathy began to tell me of someone that she watched from a distance, that she was infatuated with, that she desired. As unbelievable as it sounds now, I listened with no clue about the object of her affection or no thought of anything going beyond this weird encounter. She looked at me and asked pointedly, "Do you know who I'm talking about? I'm talking about you."

At that instant a volcano of desire erupted. Whatever sin that followed over the next three months was committed right then and there in my heart. James says, "Each one is tempted when, by his own evil desire he is dragged away and enticed. Then, after desire has conceived, it gives birth to sin; and sin, when it is full-grown, gives birth to death." (James 1:14-15) In that moment of conception, there in the lobby of a huge church on Sunday after the service, in that moment of conception, all of the characteristics of the sin that would follow were present. Just as the human embryo contains the complete genetic make-up of the adult, so the desire conceived in my heart at that moment had all of the DNA of the awful, shameful, despicable acts that would follow. I found what I had been looking for all of these years, lust.

Doris has found a writer that we both have fallen in love with, Beth Moore. She is an unbelievably gifted communicator, but more than that, she writes out of her life struggles. Her approach to dealing with them, especially the intimate parts of her story, is my guide here. In To Live Is Christ, one of her many books, she says, "Remember an important principle about sharing our former conduct. Generalizations usually are best. I try to avoid becoming specific about ungodly actions in my past. I want the listener to focus on my Savior, not my behavior. Sometimes we glorify ungodly behavior by highlighting how bad we were. This method can dishonor God, and it can dishonor the listener by stirring unnecessary mental images of sin." (To Live Is Christ, Beth Moore, pg, 187)

It is enough to say that I had an affair that lasted a few weeks. I also discovered that I had a wonderful ability to compartmentalize. I was a high profile pastor at a high profile church. I was teaching and speaking to hundreds of young adults each week, attending denominational meetings and writing articles for a national Christian magazine; and I was committing gross sin against God, the church, and my family.

After several weeks, the war in my heart was so depressing and demoralizing that it was as obvious on the outside as it was hellish on the inside. Doris confronted me with the things that she saw and I confessed, partly. I told her that I had been involved in a romantic relationship that was not physical. I begged for her forgiveness and swore, genuinely so, that I would never, ever allow such a thing to happen again. I wept true tears of sorrow and shame and prayed for God and my wife to give me another chance. Miraculously, both did.

One of the most incredible miracles of grace that God has put in my life is Doris. She, more than any human being I have ever known, modeled then and models now the compassionate heart of Christ. Her spirit may be broken. She may be wounded so deeply that she cannot breathe but she has lived a life of forgiveness, sympathy and love. I know that so much more now than I did then but on that day in Midland I saw it. She, with hurting heart and shattered sense of being loved, loved me and took me back. We held each other and sat on the couch for hours. Joshua was staying with a family in the church. We examined out relationship. We made new promises. I told half-truths. We sobbed and prayed and hugged, silently at times. And when the day was over, my marriage was salvaged and I was sure that this would never happen again.

No one, outside of the three of us, Doris, myself and Cathy, the other woman, knew for sure that the affair actually happened. And Doris did not know the whole truth. We went on with life and things seemed good.

The next few years at Midland were some of the most delightful years in our lives. The church was growing. Our ministry was increasing. I was more and more being recognized on a national level for my work. Our son Joshua was the joy of the church. Our lives abounded with friends, family and fame but the disease to please, compounded now by the pain of my past, continued to eat at me and remind me that it was all a façade and that I was worthless.

It was at that time that a call came from a destitute and dying church in Swansea, Indiana. They had no hope, no future, no money and almost no people. It was not the place that an up-and-coming, successful young minister should go to take his first job as senior pastor and continue a rising career. But I began to see this call as a way to earn God's affection. I would go to this awful place, do my penance, and thereby deserve what I longed for so much, the love of God. In October, five years after arriving at Midland, this model, mega-church, I shocked everyone by moving my pregnant wife and five year old son, to Swansea, Indiana, a church that God had forsaken.

Chapter 6

SWANSEA

Thursday is Evaluation Day at The Clinic. It says so on my schedule "Eleven to eleven-twenty AM--Evaluation." Some of the "inmates" have been here more than a week, and I sense from their uneasiness that Evaluation is not as mundane as it sounds, nor is it pleasant.

I am sitting in the waiting room working on my recovery journal. In Group this morning, we were joined by a half-dozen men from the community who are in recovery. Actually, as I sat there I realized that we were joining them. Apparently this is a weekly Twelve Step meeting and we "newbies' are allowed to sit in. It is still bizarre to hear men and women describe their addictions and the horrible choices they have made in very matter of fact tones. I get the feeling that nothing I or any of the newbies say would shock these veterans of recovery. There is something strangely comforting in that.

After group I had another session with Dr. Bowman and now I am in a session with Phillip Bell. I don't like him. Dr. Bell is the psychiatrist on staff at The Clinic. Maybe I have a preconceived distrust and dislike of him because of that. It seems less foreboding to talk to a therapist or converse with a counselor. Even seeing a psychologist is not so bad but to be treated by a psychiatrist, well, you have to be crazy to need something like that.

Dr. Bell gets right to the point and doesn't let me tell my side of the story. He forces his own interpretation on my history without letting me soften it with spin. He says. "So, you are here because you are a lust addict. You have had a number of affairs and you are having an affair now."

"Not exactly," I try to respond, "I'm still not sure that we are talking about a true addiction."

He doesn't look up. He hardly ever looks directly at me while we are talking, always down at his notes or out the window in his office. This time he just reaches behind him to his desk and picks up a white book with no name or title on the cover. He opens it to the exact page, a sign that he has done this before, and reads.

"Our experiences have revealed three aspects of our condition that commonly identify addictions: tolerance, abstinence, and withdrawal. If someone has experienced these three phenomena in some area of his or her life, that person is generally regarded as being addicted. When we apply this test to ourselves, we identify as being addicted to lust, sex, relationships, or various combinations of these---for starters." (White Book, page 30)

He looks out the window and asks me, "Has your tolerance increased so that your affairs have been progressively longer in duration and more brazen?" I can tell it is a question we both already know the answer to so he isn't expecting me to reply. "Have you gone through periods of attempted abstinence where you told yourself it would never happen again and yet it has?" Again we both are silent. "When you try to quit an affair or lust relationship did you experience symptoms of depression, anxiety and even physical illness?" It would have been more comfortable if he had finished with a, "so you see," or "that is why." Instead, the application seems so obvious that he doesn't even make it.

I feebly offer my next defense. "I wouldn't say that I have had a *number* of affairs."

"Three is a number." He doesn't look up.

At least I'm on solid ground here, "Well, the last affair ended several months ago. I am not having an affair now."

He surprises me by looking right at me. I wish he would look out the window again. "My notes say that you moved away from the place of your last affair. I would call that geographical abstinence. They also say that you have continued to talk to that person on the phone and communicate by e-mail. Look Mike, you can call that whatever you want. I really don't care what you call it but it is an ongoing affair. You are an addict. And we will be wasting our time until you start telling the whole truth all of the time, especially to yourself."

The way he punctuates *is* and *are* and *will* in that last comment, it is like three slaps to my face. I sit there in fact, with red cheeks and look out the window.

Dr. Bell looks like a beefy Al Pacino. His straight, black, hair is a tiny bit too long and a tiny bit too oily. His eyes are small and so dark that they fail to register as a distinct color and they are shaded by heavy, wild, eyebrows. His face is craggy and just on the line between handsome and not attractive. He seldom makes eye contact, and when he does, it is more of a glare than a look. He is in a helping profession but possesses an innate ability to intimidate.

"You ran from your first affair without getting help," he states bluntly. I know there is no use arguing. "Tell me about the move to Swansea."

Swansea, Indiana was everything that Midland was not. Or maybe it is the other way around. Midland was a quaint, beautiful little village in the heart of some of the most tranquil country in the world. Swansea was a dying, factory town on the edge of the steel belt. Midland was full of gingerbread cottages and whitewashed picket fences. Swansea was filled with abandoned factories and blocks of smog covered mill houses. Midland was laced with cobblestone streets lined with twinkling streetlights. Swansea was strangled with pot-hole scarred asphalt and discarded trash cans. Swansea, Indiana was not the postcard city of the Midwest.

The church in Swansea mirrored the city. It was an inner-city church that at one time must have been a light house in a bustling, productive community. As the factories closed, and the city began to die, the life seeped from the church. The old, yellow brick building sat on the middle of a city block wedged between a nursing home and a bingo lodge. Its stained glassed windows were cracked and what was left of the shrubs were overgrown and dying.

Inside, there were several places where rain had leaked through the roof and stained the ceiling. The balcony, once full of worshippers had become a storage bin for outdated hymnals and old Christmas decorations. The carpet was worn down the center aisle and between the pews so that, in some places, the cement floor peeked through the threads. A dilapidated, Baldwin organ hovered in the corner of the sanctuary and the most massive pulpit I have ever seen squatted all over the platform. It was a less than appealing place of worship, which didn't matter because there were not many people to appeal to.

The last Sunday in Midland was a wonderful day. The church planned a big send off for us and there were several thousand in the service. The next week I was the senior pastor of the church in Swansea with eighty-three in attendance. Of that number, ten were under sixty years old. Doris smiled sweetly through the entire service and then went home, laid on the couch, and cried. She did that every Sunday for the first two months.

A few months after we moved to Swansea our second son, Jacob, was born. He came out with red hair and a big grin on his face. The day after he was born, Doris put on her best gown, we fixed Jacob up with a bow, (his mother's idea,) and we sat in the hospital room and waited for people from the church to come by and visit. No one came. Late in the day a family from Midland drove all the way down to see us. Doris smiled sweetly and when they left she laid on the bed and cried.

Joshua was almost five when Jacob was born. He was quiet and reserved like his mother, and such a compliant little boy, a perfect child. One day I looked at Doris and said, "You know, we have this parenting thing down pat. We are perfect parents." God heard that and laughed and laughed and sent us Jacob.

My office looked out over a small courtyard at the church. In the center of the courtyard was a large, blue fountain that someone had given in memory of a saintly, dead, grandmother years earlier. One of the men came every week and cleaned and polished the fountain meticulously. The rest of the church was decaying but that fountain was spectacular. It was a sacred place for the old people of the church.

Jacob was about two when one Sunday after church I looked out my office window to see a crowd of senior citizens standing in dismay around the fountain. I hurried out to see what was going on. Jacob had stripped completely naked and was doing the back stroke in the fountain. Doris went home and laid on the couch and cried.

In spite of that, the anointing of God settled on that little, downtown church in Swansea. One Saturday night a few men in the church came to pray. We walked through the sanctuary and asked God to fill the pews the next day. On Sunday morning eighty new people were in the worship service, nearly as many new people as old. They stayed and the congregation never looked back. Before long, more than five-hundred people were crammed into the dingy, old, sanctuary each week. They filled the balcony. They sat in the window sills. They overflowed the parking lot.

I have never known why the churches that I served grew so rapidly. I always felt that if the people really knew how inadequate I was, no one would come. I have come to believe that when God is ready, He blesses the ministry, often in spite of the minister. It certainly made me aware that "success" in the church is not always a sure sign that the leader is living a godly life. There were wonderful, holy, pastor friends of mine that prayed for me and their churches did not grow. And there were times when my church did grow and I was as far from God as I could imagine being.

As the church began to grow, the denomination began to recognize my work. I was elected to state and national offices. I was asked to serve on college boards and denominational committees. The church (and I) rose to prominence in the city, the state and the denomination. I was asked to travel to other churches to tell them the secret of spiritual success. All of that felt good but at the same time, the accolades only served to widen the gulf between who I thought people assumed me to be and who I thought I really was. Every honor drove me to a deeper sense of panic at the thought of being found out. Late at night, with only my wife's breathing breaking the silence, I would weep and ask God to make me into the image everyone expected me to be. Not into His image but the image I thought people around me wanted.

One day an elderly, saintly pastor friend called me aside at a state meeting and gave me a warning. He said, "Mike, the church will use you until you are an empty shell and then they will throw you away and wonder what happened to you. They will make you so busy and involve you on so many boards and committees that you forget to take time for the things that matter, loving God and loving your family. Then when it all falls apart they will move on to the next successful young pastor." I listened to his prophetic admonition and chalked it up to the bitterness of an old man. I look back now, and marvel at how accurate he was.

The tremendous growth forced us to buy property and build at Swansea. Months turned into years of planning, fund raising, designing and finally building. To the church work and national work I now added building committees, finance meetings, "bathroom brainstorming design teams" and "moms-mad-about-the-new-nursery advisory groups." New people were coming to the church every week. I was on the run all of the time, trying to stay ahead of the curve. I always felt less than capable, always felt like a phony and was always desperately afraid to fail. My disease to please was raging. I was a circus juggler, spinning plates. I had to keep everybody happy so that somebody would like me and not let anybody see me for the nobody I really was.

In the fall of my seventh year at Swansea, we dedicated the new church. It was a state of the art, cutting edge, high tech facility. There were basketball courts, in ground baptismal pools and beautiful bathrooms where the paper towels came out automatically. We had rear screen projectors, top notch stage lighting and two nurseries staffed by the now "moms-happy-about-the-new-nursery advisory group." The dedication service was attended by national church leaders, state senators, former pastors, the mayor and hundreds of people who had come to know Christ through the ministry of that church over the last seven years. Our church staff was excellent and proud. Doris looked radiant in her new church dedication dress. Josh and Jacob were spit shined to a tee. And I was emotionally and spiritually exhausted.

Dr. Bell interjects, "Some of the Twelve Step material warns about letting yourself get susceptible to "acting out" your addiction. It uses the acronym HALT. Do not let yourself become Hungry, Angry, Lonely or Tired. It is at these times that addiction is strongest." I agree by nodding. I was all of those and more by the time we dedicated the new building.

One day I was visiting a young, single mother who had gone through a great tragedy in her life. The church had been ministering to her in her time of grief and I had often prayed with her and her children. On this day I asked, with no hidden meaning or agenda, "What can I do for you today?" She responded, "You can be a clone. I need someone exactly like you." Just as before in Midland, at that moment a dam of restraint burst in my heart and brain. All of the frustration and fear and feeling of unlovability came gushing through. The worthless, unloved little boy in me screamed with glee, "At last, you have found someone who will love you." And sin was full born in my soul.

I do not know how to describe it better. I understand now the process and the spiritual failures that led up to that moment. But I can only say that one second, having an affair, being unfaithful to my wife and my God, was the last thing I could ever imagine, much less do. The very next second, I had given myself to it, not actually but emotionally, so that the deed was all but inevitable. While physical contact did not happen for several weeks, in my inner person, I committed adultery that very moment.

Dr. Bell is looking at me again. There is a long silence as I can think of nothing else to say and he does not feel the need to say anything. Finally he opens the same, well worn, white book. He reads in a soft voice, almost a whisper, "We became true addicts: sex with self, promiscuity, adultery, dependency relationships and more fantasy. We got it through the eyes; we bought it, we sold it, we traded it, we gave it away. We were addicted to the intrigue, the tease, the forbidden. The only way we knew to be free of it was to do it. 'Please connect with me and make me whole!' we cried with outstretched arms. Lusting after the Big Fix, we gave away our power to others." (<u>White Book</u>, page *v*)

I am sobbing as he continues, "The insanity of your actions testify to the fact that you are an addict. The obsessive-compulsive behavior of the event you have just described can only be attributed to a person who is out of control and hopelessly enslaved." I can't look him in the face. I study, through hot tears, the tattered corner of the upholstered sofa I am sitting on. I notice it is stained and worn and pick at the loose threads. I wonder how many people have picked at this spot before. Dr. Bell says nothing else. There is no consoling, no comforting. He has brought me to a conclusion and that is his job.

The door opens quietly behind us and Carl Rivers says, "It's time for Evaluation."

Chapter 7

EVALUATION

Dr. Dunning is an "enigma wrapped in a conundrum." He is everyone's grandpa, a kind and gentle man with flowing, gray hair and an easy smile that crinkles his face from the edge of his mouth to the corner of his eyes. He is not unusually tall, maybe six feet, but when he enters a room he seems larger than life and the whole crowd gravitates toward him. He has a quick sense of humor and makes idle conversation just as well about NASCAR or petunias. I like him a lot until he starts to tell the truth.

The entire staff at The Clinic is fiercely committed to the truth and it is obvious that it begins with the founder and director, Dr. Dunning. He seems incapable of shading or softening the facts in anyway, even to protect the feelings of his patient. From the first conversation I have with him over the phone it is apparent that he will not engage, nor allow me to engage, in hyperbole. He is the original *Dragnet* guy: "Just the facts, ma'am, only the facts." This is especially clear during Evaluation.

His office is large, three times as large as any other counselor's office at The Clinic. It has an ordinary wooden desk in the corner with his name on a gold plate, "Dr. Roy Dunning, Ph.D." The walls are lined with plaques and pictures of Dr. Dunning and photo-op dignitaries. But the dominant theme in his office is space. There are a few small sofas scatter around the walls and a stack of metal folding chairs standing by the door. Other than that there is just space, an open carpeted area that is waiting to be filled with groups, circles and staff meetings. In this utilitarian expanse, Dr. Dunning, and the rest of the staff, tell the truth.

When I enter his office, during Evaluation, the folding chairs are set up in a large circle and filled with the therapists from the clinic. Two dozen men and women sit around the room with Dr. Dunning behind his desk. Andie Bowman is there and Dr. Bell. Jerry Carlson and Kay Heinz sit beside each other directly across from the door. Every counselor I have seen, and some I have not, turn to acknowledge me as Carl Rivers leads me into the room and then turn back to their coffee and conversation.

Carl motions for me to take a seat in one of the folding chairs, not in the circle but in a corner opposite Dr. Dunning's desk and conspicuously on the outside of the group of counselors. He doesn't sit but remains standing and picks up his legal pad. He clears his throat and addresses the room. They immediately give him their full attention and I immediately disappear. The conversation begins with me as the subject and not a single person glances at me or seems aware that I am present while they discuss the most intimate and horrific details of my life.

"He is a practiced liar," says one counselor. "Telling lies has become a common defense mechanism for him."

"He seems unwilling to admit the depth of the problem," says Dr. Bell. "He still has to be convinced that he is an addict."

"We are about half-way through his history and he seems to write himself as either the hero or the victim in every story," adds Carl Rivers. "I don't see him yet taking responsibility for his own actions."

One by one, around the room, each therapist that I have talked to reports on our conversations in very clinical and, it seems to me, critical terms. The counselors I have not talked to, ask questions and make suggestions, all with no apparent awareness that I am sitting right here and that they are turning over every rock of my most sordid deeds. I have been warned against arguing, or in fact, speaking out at all during the Evaluation. I sit here in a pool of dismay with waves of frustration washing over me. I am learning what it means to be absolutely powerless.

Dr. Dunning sits behind his desk, expressionless. He is the first person I talked to after Doris left. He was so kind and helpful in arranging my admittance to the clinic. He suggested books to read while I waited for the time to arrive. He spoke in soft tones over the phone about the flight and where I might stay while I was out here. I expected him to come to my defense now, but he sits with his hands together, fingertips against fingertips and his mouth resting on his thick index fingers, waiting for the last therapist to speak. "This afternoon," he says, "I will go over Mike's MMPI with him." He offers no further explanation but each counselor looks satisfied as if whatever that is will do whatever they expect needs to be done.

Without another word, Carl Rivers opens the door and I know that I am supposed to leave. There is no "see you later" or "thanks for coming." My presence is no longer desired and I am to leave. I walk alone down the corridor that leads back to the waiting room but, my mind is somewhere else. This event is so much like the meeting with the state minister's board after Swansea. It ended the same way.

The affair in Swansea lasted for several months. It is enough to say that sin always turns out the same way. What starts out as some kind of ecstatic pleasure and an escape from reality eventually becomes a hellish trap from which there seems to be no release. Romance turns into a pathetic cycle of acting out, then shame and guilt that can only be relieved by acting out. As a minister the whirlpool of destruction was even more powerful. I wanted to stop but, if I stopped, she would tell, and if she told I would lose everything, so I continued lying, now to my wife <u>and</u> the other woman, on a path that could only lead to losing everything. Yet even that explanation is too simple because in the midst of desperately wanting to stop, the addict in me desperately wanted to keep going. The First Step describes it as being "powerless over lust" and says "our life is unmanageable."

Secret sin doesn't remain a secret. One day one of my staff members came into my office and began to weep. He told me what he was not supposed to tell me, that I was being investigated by the state minister's board and that they were ready to bring me up on charges. It was a few days before Christmas and the snow and ice that covered the frozen, Indiana city squeezed its way into my heart. Terror and embarrassment and panic and anger rose up in me in artic blasts. My thoughts raced. My heart pounded as I drove home to tell my wife that what I said would never happen again had happened again.

I don't know why Doris stayed. I only know that she, broken and shattered in her own heart, was then and is now, the most perfect human example of the grace of God I can ever imagine. She was not "alright." She did not take my hand and say, "I forgive you. We will get through it." Over the next months, she cried and screamed and sat in silence and turned away from me, but she stayed. We stumbled through Christmas, determined that the boys, still children, would not know.

We drove north the day after New Years to the state office in Miranda. The state overseer met us at the door and literally fell on me and wept. He hugged us in an awkward, forced way and sobbed uncontrollably into my chest for several seconds. We took our seats in front of his desk, he behind it and Doris and I held hands nervously and asked him what we could do. The state overseer was an ex-military noncom with a by-the-book approach to all things, even grace. He quoted the disciplinary procedure of the church from memory and then turned to me with these instructions, "You are to go home and pack up your office, your books and any possessions you have at the church. On Sunday morning you will call a special meeting of the church to state what you have done and that you are resigning as pastor of the church. Then you will leave. You are to have no contact with anyone in the church. Neither you nor your family are to attend another service at the church. We will contact you in a few months to tell you what to do next." Doris and I walked alone, back out to the car and drove south to Swansea and began to pack.

In a few months I was called to a meeting of the state minister's board. As he opened the door completely I saw that the entire state minister's board was assembled around a huge, walnut, conference table. They sat stoically and watched as I entered the room without actually looking at me or acknowledging my presence. The state overseer took his place at the end of the table. He had prepared a dossier from the investigation and a copy lay before each member of the board. He motioned for me to sit in a wooden chair, conspicuously outside of the group, and began the meeting.

He recounted the "facts," some of them accurate and some of them not, and then told the board that I had confessed and resigned under pressure. I did not say anything. Instead, the state overseer quoted again from the disciplinary manual of the church and asked if there were any questions. A few men asked a few questions, of him, not of me. The probation period to reenter the ministry was to be no less than five years. During that time I would come once a year to a meeting of this board and report my progress. I would meet with another pastor once a month for the first year. I was not allowed any involvement in any church, in anyway. I could not testify, take up the offering or sing in the choir. With that he stood up and opened the door. I could tell that my presence was no longer needed or desired.

We moved to be near our family in middle Tennessee shortly after that, and once a year, I would get in the car and drive north to Miranda, Indiana and the meeting of the state minister's board.

The next five years in Tennessee were good years. I started a business and worked long hours to get it off the ground. We bought a small house on the edge of a nice community not far from Nashville and threw ourselves into our sons. Joshua entered high school and discovered an athletic prowess that must have come from his mother. He played baseball and basketball and much of our calendar was filled with games and practices and sports camps.

Jacob found music. His God given talent certainly was passed down from his mother and music became a passion for him. Saxophone. Bass guitar. Piano. Guitar. Now to our calendar we added private lessons, concerts and state contests. Both boys excelled and seemed to be healthy and fairly well oblivious to the failure of my past. On occasion a question would come up about Swansea: "Why don't we ever go back to visit? Why did we move so fast?" Doris and I usually brushed it off and the boys seemed fine with life the way it was.

We began to attend a wonderful, little church in our town. The pastor was about my age and we became close friends. After a few months I took him to lunch and told him as much of the story as I could bring myself to tell. He accepted it with kindness and sympathy and, as far as I could tell, never thought of it again in the years we spent in his congregation. Pastor Jeff's sermons were always encouraging and full of mercy. He was a good man and a good pastor and my family grew closer to God under his ministry. I began to be more aware than ever of the joy of the church as opposed to The Church. Whatever God intended the church to be in terms of ministry to sinners is certainly best accomplished Sunday by Sunday when the 'band of believers' come together. The things that happen in the larger, worldwide church are not so much the things of God.

Doris and I began to heal. I worked hard at being a good husband and a good father. I felt if I could be attentive enough, send enough cards, attend enough ball games, help with the dishes enough, I could make up for the offenses of the past. I threw myself into the business and worked hard to provide an above average income for my family. We laughed a lot and thought about the past less and less. Once a year I would make my trek to Miranda, beyond that I had no contact with anyone from that part of my life.

The unspoken goal for us was to get back into the ministry. I think we both felt that doing so would be the ultimate vindication for what I had done and would meet a need that constantly burned within me, that is the need to help people. In my mind, a return to the ministry also meant an opportunity to earn my way back into favor with God and with my peers. In spite of the outward peace of those years, the inner disease to please was still very much alive. And it helped each time I met with the state minister's board. I was able to tell them exactly what they wanted to hear.

At the end of five years, I met the board for the last time. They asked me to see a licensed counselor for a final evaluation. It was the only counselor I was asked to see in the whole five years of recovery. I met a therapist in Nashville who talked with me for forty-five minutes. I don't remember his name but when we were finished he faxed a form letter to the state overseer saying that I was fully recovered from whatever it was that I was supposed to be recovered from. A month later I received a letter in the mail welcoming me back into the ranks of ministers. The long struggle was over and I knew I would never put my family through that again.

My reverie is interrupted by Dr. Rivers. The evaluations are over and it is time to get back to work. It is just after lunch and time for my daily session with him. He comes to the waiting room to get me and we walk down the hall to his office. As we do we pass the office of Dr. Dunning, the door is open and I can see that all of the folding chairs have been folded up and stand in a stack next to the door again. The walls are lined with small sofas and the open space is ready for the next event. It is as if we were never in there at all.

Chapter 8

HARRISON

Carl Rivers is pushing and I am fighting back. His goal has been to get my entire case history down this week. Each day we pick up where we left off the day before and now, at week's end, he is trying to bring this part of the process to a close. Normally, I would be just as eager as he is to finish this up and move on. My addict self has learned to tell partial truths and then sweep the whole thing under the carpet so that I can minimize the pain. But this afternoon I am pouting. I feel like Carl abandoned me in the Evaluation. I think he could have stood up for me a little bit so I resist his efforts to draw more of the story out.

"The last time we talked you were leaving Swansea and moving back to Tennessee," he says. "How did your family respond to that?"

"They did fine," I jab. "We really didn't tell the boys anything and they seemed to be okay."

"Why didn't you tell them what was going on?" Carl asks.

"They were young; we just felt it was the right way to handle it."

I know he wants more, but I am being a baby. My life is in shambles. I am desperate for help. This guy is charging me two hundred dollars an hour. And I am having a pity party because he didn't stand up for me in front of a room full of people I will never see again.

Carl smiles at me and stands and walks across his office to a small, wooden bookshelf in the corner. He picks up a worn, blue paperback and thumbs through it. I can see him mentally checking off passages until he settles on the right one. He reads, "It is plain that a life which includes deep resentment leads only to futility and unhappiness. To the precise extent that we permit these, do we squander the hours that might have been worthwhile. ... If we were to live, we had to be free of anger. The grouch and the brainstorm were not for us. They may be the dubious luxury of normal men, but for the alcoholics these things are poison." (AA Big Book, pg. 66)

Carl sits back down and adds, "I your case, *addict* is a better word." He picks up his ever present legal pad and says, "Tell me about getting back into the ministry."

About a month after being reinstated I received a call from a church leader in another denomination asking me to "fill in" at a problem church that had been without a pastor for some time. The first Sunday I went to preach at Harrison, Alabama, there were thirty-five people present and the sanctuary was pretty full. Harrison was a tiny, country church that had been surprised by a city growing up around it.

The red brick building sat in the middle of a field of ragweed and dandelions on an Alabama hillside. A quarter of a mile away was the interstate and a large metropolitan community. But on this little hillside in Harrison there was just God and the church and the great outdoors. (And I'm not absolutely sure that God was there.) To say that it was a dying church is a generous exaggeration. Harrison was dead but no one had performed the funeral yet.

In its nearly one hundred year history many families had come to raise their children in the safety of the church. Almost universally, as the children became young adults, they drifted away, either leaving their faith altogether, or moving on to the more glamorous and entertaining big city churches down the road. All that was left was the handful of gray-headed, old couples that had seen their children move away and their friends pass away. Like a stagnant pool that has felt the life evaporate from it, the "blue hairs" at Harrison had become toxic and lifeless. They were the people that listened to me that first Sunday at Harrison.

The service was plain, two songs and a poem, and I preached a simple message on encouraging one another. The next day my phone rang and the chairman of the board said they wanted me to become their pastor.

My last Sunday as associate pastor at Midland several thousand people had been present. My last Sunday as pastor in Swansea there had been several hundred present. Now I was invited to become the pastor of just "several." I was beginning to see a pattern. But it seemed like the right thing to do. The church was a world I was most comfortable with and I felt this small church might be my way of getting back in God's good grace, so I accepted the call, and my wife and I and Josh and Jacob became the proud parsonage family of the booming church in Harrison. The church welcomed us with a bouquet of flowers and huge a number of casseroles in Tupperware containers. They told us we could keep the containers.

At first, the ministry at Harrison was just a job. I saw it as a way to get back into the fellowship of the church world. If I spent a couple of years here and performed respectably, then a *real* church would see that and offer me a position. It was also a way to alleviate any fears that Doris might have about being back in this role. Surely, the things that had happened before, in large churches, would never happen in this tiny fishbowl of a church where everybody kept an eye on everybody.

We did not relocate to Harrison but kept our house in middle Tennessee and commuted each weekend. I would visit the people on Saturday, hold services on Sunday, have business or planning meetings Sunday afternoon, and we would drive back home, exhausted, ready to get up and go to work on Monday. The term is bi-vocational pastor, which means someone who is trying to hold down two full-time jobs and not doing very well at either one.

Almost immediately the little church at Harrison began to grow. New people seemed to appear every Sunday, young adults returning to worship with their parents, young families that were looking for an exciting place to get their kids involved in church. I told the congregation one Sunday, when there were about seventy there, that if we ever had two-hundred people in worship I would preach from the roof of the church.

Within a few weeks, they invited and begged and crammed two-hundred-and-twelve people into a sanctuary that was built to seat eighty. By the next Sunday the men had built a platform on the peak of the church roof. The whole congregation gathered in the parking lot and I climbed, with fear and trembling, to what I was sure would be my death, and preached one of the shortest sermons I have ever preached. Television and newspaper reporters were there and the next thing I knew, the church at Harrison was on the map.

We added a second service on Sunday morning and then a third on Saturday night. The children would meet in the basement and the teens in a tent on the parking lot. Still the sanctuary was packed to overflowing every service with people literally sitting in the window sills and on the floor. There was an incredible sense of joy and the presence of God seemed to settle over this country hillside. I preached on grace and God's love and people came from all over. It was a great time to be in the church.

I gave up my business in middle Tennessee and Doris and I and Jacob moved to Harrison. Josh was attending a college not far away and came for weekends. Doris played the piano, Jacob played the bass in the praise band, and Josh worked with the teens. We were the ideal parsonage family. And the church was the ideal church, enthusiastic, energetic and visionary.

God sent all kinds of people to the church at Harrison. There were doctors and farmers, teachers and mechanics, the upper class and families right out of the projects. The people loved us and loved each other and God blessed us. Everyone was welcome and everyone felt a part. And nobody felt more of a part than Art.

Art was thirty-five or so and unemployed. He lived in a low income apartment with his sister and her husband, not far from the church and walked to church every day. Not every Sunday.

Every day. He would knock on the door of my office and come in just to talk. He talked about the weather, sports, the number of cars on the highway, what he had for supper the night before. He just talked. And he smelled. To be perfectly honest, Art was less than clean and after a long walk on a hot summer day, he pretty much filled my office with an aroma that was not fragrant.

I began to give Art jobs around the church. On Monday he would straighten up all of the hymnals in the sanctuary. On Tuesday he would pick up trash in the basement. On Wednesday he would set up folding chairs in the fellowship hall. And on Thursday, Art would fold the bulletins. In the South we would say that Art wasn't playing with a full deck, but I liked Art, and he loved me.

I would take him home with me for supper some nights and Doris and Jacob would hold their breath and hug him like a long, lost brother. One night I asked Jacob to take Art back to his sister's apartment after supper. On the ride back Jacob asked, "Art, have you ever been saved?" To which Art replied, "No." So Jacob proceeded to lead Art to Jesus, in the car, on the way home.

One Sunday afternoon we planned a baptismal service. There were dozens of new people who wanted to be baptized in this exciting, growing church. We made all of the preparations for that big day. The men cleaned out the old baptistry that was filled with Vacation Bible School supplies and paint. The ladies made white robes out of old bed sheets. Friends and neighbors were invited. It was huge, a big day of celebration for the church.

Two things happened right at the beginning of that day that should have been a premonition of things to come. First, the dilapidated, old heater in the baptistry gave out. And second, Art said he wanted to be baptized.

The service began with singing and shouting. The sanctuary was overflowing and the baptistry nearly was. We placed a microphone in front of the pool so that the congregation could hear the testimony of the new saints. The curtain pulled back and I stepped gingerly into the baptismal tank. It was cold. I don't mean, just room temperature, kind of chilly, takes-a-minute-to-get-used-to it cold. I mean, gasp-for-air when-your-feet-touch-the-water, cold.

I put on a brave face, climbed in and looked back up the steps. There stood the first candidate to be baptized, in all of his glory, Art. He had decided not to wear a robe. Instead, Art had on the brightest, tackiest, Hawaiian swimming trunks I have ever seen and a dingy, Budweiser T-shirt. He took one step into the pool and let loose a string of profanity that would have embarrassed a sailor.

I finally got him quieted down and led him on into the pool. Now Art was a big guy, well over six feet and close to three hundred pounds. I am not. Baptism is about surrender; Art decided not to surrender but to fight it instead. I tried to put him under and he began to flail. The more I'd push, the bigger he would get. It looked like the finals of the Olympic water polo contest. Waves were rolling over the baptistery. The curtains were dripping. And when it was over, I am not sure who baptized whom but Jacob came up and gave Art a giant, soaking wet hug. It was a good day.

Sometime later we had a youth choir pass through and ask to give a concert at our little church. It was a Sunday night in July and the temperature was soaring. That afternoon the bus pulled up after a three-hour trip and forty teenagers got out and headed for the bathrooms. By the time the service began there were two-hundred sweating people jammed into a building built for eighty. There also were forty teens and two-hundred people using two bathrooms built for, well, two.

Just as the service began, both bathrooms stopped up, filled up, backed up and spilled over. Sewage seeped under the doors, down the halls, over the river and through the woods. There was a sweet, sweet spirit in that place but not a sweet, sweet smell. We opened the windows, turned the fans on full blast, and forty teens sang for an hour without ever taking a breath.

The leaders of the church decided it was time to build a new building.

To build a new church building is a daunting task for everyone involved but especially for the pastor. Try as I might to stay removed from the process, my days and nights began to be filled with color committees, zoning meetings, finance meetings and general, all-around busy stuff. I became bi-vocational again, part pastor and part construction superintendent.

We hired the same company that had built the building in Swansea and they built the same style building. Beautiful sanctuary that would seat hundreds, a full court gymnasium, grand nurseries, a café in the narthex complete with cappuccino machine, and an automatic paper towel dispenser in the bathroom. (How did Jesus ever reach people without an automatic paper towel dispenser?)

The strain of a two-year building project, the pressure of constantly meeting the needs of hundreds of new people, and the same old feelings of unlovability began to take its toll. I was working harder and praying less. I spent more time at the office than I did with my family. I took more of the weight on my own shoulders and placed less trust in God. All of the familiar feelings of inadequacy and worthlessness came flooding right back in and I was ripe for the fall.

One afternoon, a young adult lady came into my office and said, "My marriage is bad. I want a husband just like you." I was hooked. In a few weeks the mental images that my addiction created became actual events. Almost without thinking, I was on a binge of sickness, sin and self-destruction.

The first affair lasted a few weeks. The second lasted a few months. This time it was over a year. The stranglehold of addiction was unimaginable. I would wake up in the middle of the night in a terrified sweat, go out into the garage and scream for God to kill me and deliver me from this "body of death" as St. Paul called it. In the morning, when the sun came up I would be on the phone arranging another clandestine meeting. I was dying, emotionally, spiritually and, even physically, I was dying.

Carl stops me in the middle of a sentence. He puts down his legal pad and, instead of looking at me, closes his eyes. Without warning or explanation he begins to pray. "God, Mike is on the verge of being honest. Help him to push through. Grant him the serenity to accept the things he cannot change, the courage to change the things he can, and the wisdom to know the difference."

With that Carl opens the now familiar, and still nameless, white book. "Mike," he whispers, "This is what I hear you saying. You were dead if you quit and dead if you didn't. It is crucial for you to understand that what you have just described is not unique to you."

And then he read, "Prior to our recovery, it was impossible for any of us to comprehend or accept the true nature of our condition. ... Our diseased attitude is an irresistible force driving us away from others, ourselves, and God and into our addictions. ... And the insanity of our delusion damns us to a condition where truth about ourselves cannot penetrate. ... Had we ever glimpsed the truth for a moment, the torment would have been greater than we could bear. Thus, the illness *must* perpetuate itself, both within and without. To stop means we must face the truth about ourselves, and that is like the very threat of death. But unless we do stop and face the truth about ourselves, we remain in death." (White Book, page 56)

Tears are burning scalding rivulets down my face. I try to speak but can't. The intense days and hours at the clinic are coming to an explosive head within me and I don't trust myself to open my mouth.

Carl speaks for me. "I want you to go to group. After that," he says, "Dr. Dunning will meet with you." And then Carl does something he has not done until that moment. He puts his arms around my shoulder and walks me to the door.

Chapter 9

INTERVENTION

We attend Group two or three times a day at the clinic. Every morning we meet at seven or seven-thirty AM. Most days we eat boxed lunches during group. On some days we have group late in the evening. There are usually a dozen of us. I call us inmates. We come from all walks of life and all over the country.

Every group begins the same. We recite the Serenity Prayer, "God, Grant me the serenity to accept the things I cannot change, the courage to change the things I can, and the wisdom to know the difference." And then we go around the room and tell our first names and why we are here. "Hi, my name is Mike and I am a sex addict." To which the group responds, "Hi, Mike."

Each story is different, different ages, different socio-economic levels, even different genders. But somehow everything we hear sounds familiar. We all recognize something of ourselves in the facts and failures of our fellow "inmates." We feel unloved and unlovely. We hurt those who try to love us. We build impenetrable walls of lies and deceit to protect ourselves from the very thing we desire most, intimacy.

The repetition of both hearing and reciting our stories so often has a numbing effect on me. "My name is Mike." ("Hi, Mike.") "I am a sex addict. I am here because I have had a series of affairs, nearly destroying my wife. I have lost my family, my career, my home." "That's good, Mike. Does anybody know what we are having for lunch today?" We discuss our failures as if we are commenting on the score of last night's baseball game.

It is not that we have become immune from the pain that we have caused ourselves and others. The fact of the matter is, by repeating over and over again our offenses, we have come to own them. We are finally beginning to believe what is true and not what we have made up about ourselves. The choices we have made and the actions we have taken have had a devastating effect on everyone around us. We are addicts.

This afternoon, our second meeting of the day, Group is more somber than usual. One of the inmates is gone. Mark left after Evaluation today. He couldn't take it and instead of going to his next therapy session he packed his bag and went home. There is an empty chair in the circle where he sat just this morning. This morning he said, "Hi, my name is Mark." ("Hi, Mark.") "I am a sex addict and I am going to get help." And this afternoon, he is not here.

I think we are somber because his absence reminds us all of how fragile we are in this recovery process. I think, also, I am somber because I have considered quitting myself. Facing the shame, being forced to be truthful about my condition, coming to grips with the consequences of my actions is almost more than I can bear, especially hour after hour, day after day. It feels, at times, like there is no hope and the pain of being honest is too much.

Charles is beside me. "Hi, my name is Charles." (Hi, Charles.) "I'm here because I am a sex addict." He begins to tell his story again but I am not listening. I am thinking of another circle that I sat in a few months ago.

At the end of a year of hell in Harrison, my family had endured all that they could. Doris, my beautiful, petite wife, had lost fifteen pounds and looked like a cancer patient. Joshua had left the church, his college grades were slipping and his usually joyful face reflected an inner dismay. Jacob, the fixer, was working overtime to entertain everyone, to keep us all happy, to hold us all together. And I, immersed in my disease, refused to see.

Doris and I had argued over the "situation" often over the last few months--she accusing, me denying. She had gone to church leaders but I was so adept at deception that they began to think she had an emotional problem. The boys, Josh and Jacob, tried to confront me but I sidestepped and shuffled until they were off balance and not sure what to believe. And the church kept growing, surely evidence that everything was all right.

One afternoon, I walked out of my office and ran into our state overseer coming in. Reverend Lowry was an administrator, a good one, I am sure, but an administrator nonetheless. He didn't have the stomach for challenge or confrontation. As long as the ship was upright and making headway, why rock the boat. Doris had talked to him on more than one occasion about her suspicions. He would pray with her, promise to look into it, and go back to shuffling papers and filling out reports. And in his defense, when he did question me about her suspicions, I lied.

I can only assume that on this day, she had been desperate enough that he came to see me. "Let's go over to the church, Mike," he said. Our offices were located in an administrative building across the parking lot from the church. We walked quickly and silently over asphalt parking spaces and into the beautiful narthex of the church at Harrison. Down the hall a light was on in one of the classrooms. Lowry steered me that way.

I entered the classroom from the darkened hallway and saw a ring of chairs forming a half circle in the center of the room. Maybe ten chairs, they were partially occupied by my family.

Doris sat directly across the room. She looked nervous and very sad. Her eyes were dark and sunken and I had not noticed before that her cheekbones were so pronounced that they cast shadows on her lower face. Joshua and Jacob sat beside each other to my right. In any other setting, they would have looked comical, they were so scared. They had become tall, handsome young men, Joshua nearly through college and Jacob late in high school. But now they sat there fidgeting like fifth graders called before the principal for cheating on a math test. To my left sat my sister and brother-in-law. Her eyes were red and swollen, the obvious residual effect of a tearful journey to our little town. My brother-in-law had the desperate look of a man who would rather be anywhere else in the world right at that moment.

As I took all of this in, Reverend Lowry closed the door behind me and asked me to have a seat. "Mike," he said in his best administrator voice, "We are here because your family is concerned about you and wants to help you put a stop to your actions." Looking back, it would have been more appropriate for him to say, "Hi, my name is Phil." ("Hi, Phil.")

For the next two hours, I sat before the people that I loved more than anything in the world, the only people who really had any chance of loving me, and "lied like a dog," to use a Southern expression. Doris told what she thought was happening. I countered with plausible explanations. Josh and Jacob wept and described how they felt. I responded with half-truths and insincere apologies. My sister got down-right mad and screamed at me. I smiled and spouted spiritual-sounding platitudes. For every attack, I had a counterpunch. To every plea, I offered a false assurance.

They wept. I wept. They accused. I denied. They begged. I promised. And when it was all over, I had lied well enough to relieve just a little of their pain and convince them that everything would be okay. I am not sure what they all thought when we left that classroom. I know that I thought I had dodged a bullet, avoided a direct hit one more time, and that we would all make it. I also was sure that I would end this affair, secretly, and never, never, never, do anything like this again.

The administrator hugged us all. My family filed out without looking at me and left me sitting alone in the classroom. I put my face in my hands and sobbed for what seemed like hours. I pleaded with God to change me. I promised Him I would be different. I assured Him that nothing like this would happen again. I lied to God and hoped He would believe me.

It was dark when I finally walked back across the parking lot to my office. There was a note on my desk to call a friend, a state overseer in Florida. I picked up the phone, still numb, and dialed his number. We talked for a half-hour or so and, when we hung up, I had accepted a church in Miami, Florida. God had worked every-thing out. I knew we would be okay. We were going to move.

The topic in Group today is honesty. We have gone around the circle of chairs and commented on our inability to be honest, and the absolute necessity to do so. I told the story of my "interven-tion" and watched as nearly every person in the room nodded with recognition. How incredible that I was finally being totally honest in a room full of addicts that I had only known for a few days, telling them about lying to a room full of people that had loved me their whole life.

Dr. Bell was in Group today. He spoke up, reading from the white book, "Denial becomes woven into the fabric of our being. By refusing to listen to that still small voice within, we begin by denying we are hurting ourselves. For this lie to persist, denial must pervert the reality of ourselves and others and turns into blindness. We become unwilling and finally unable to see the truth about ourselves." (White Book, page 36)

We all agree. At last we are being honest. We are seeing the truth about ourselves. There is no room in the life of an addict for half-truths and exaggerations. The whole truth, and nothing but the truth, is the only possible way to survive. If Mark had done that he would still be here. I am so proud of myself that I nearly sprain my shoulder trying to pat myself on the back. "No more denial for me," I think. "I am ready to be honest and to have others be honest with me."

Carl comes to the door. "Mike, Dr. Dunning is ready to see you now."

Chapter 10

MIAMI

The corridors in the clinic are tiled with Arizona sandstone. I imagine they are easy to keep clean and never wear out but they make a loud clacking when you walk on them. It seems especially loud this afternoon as I make my way to Dr. Dunning's office. Behind the closed doors that line the hallways I hear the murmur of counseling sessions in progress and wish I was in one of them. I don't know why but I dread facing Dr. Dunning.

At his door I pause, not sure whether to knock or go on in. Carl said he was ready for me but I'm not clear about what that means. I finally reach a mental compromise and knock as I open the door.

Dr. Dunning is sitting behind his desk, across the expanse of open space in his office. His walnut desk is very neat and orderly, a sign of something, I'm sure, with a leather bound ink blotter in perfect center and a framed picture of his family on the corner. Behind him is a wall-size bookshelf and on the center shelf, at eye level, are the dozen or so books that bear his name as author, Dr. Roy Dunning, Ph.D. The folding chairs are stacked by the door. Without looking up, he gestures for me to sit on one of the couches. I sit, shuffle about to get less uncomfortable, and look around the room while I wait for him to start our session. I read the plaques on the wall, college and graduate school diplomas. He has a degree from a seminary that I am familiar with. There is a picture of him, smiling broadly, with his arms around two people that must be his parents.

I think Dr. Dunning is in his mid-sixties. It's not so much that he looks mid-sixty, he has one of those faces that could be forty or eighty, but the plaques on the wall must have taken some time to earn. I guess mid-sixties. I know he started The Clinic more than two decades ago and his son is a senior counselor here. Mid-sixties sounds about right. His background is in the ministry and he grew up in the same denomination that I did. A few times, since I have been here, we have talked casually about common acquaintances.

I suddenly realize that I have been staring at his face while trying to determine his age and, for the last few moments, he has been staring back at mine. He doesn't smile or frown but looks intently at me until I drop my gaze and try to determine the age of the carpet at my feet.

When the silence has gone on long enough to stretch beyond uneasy, Dr. Dunning clears his throat and speaks softly. "How has your week been?

I don't think he is making idle conversation. I believe there is a point to his question, so I try to describe my progress and impress him with my earnest effort to get better. I talk about the counselors and the approach each one is taking. I tell him about Group and the insights I have gained from the other "inmates." I comment on the assigned reading I have been doing and the things I have written in my journal. I rattle all of that off in about ninety seconds and then, I realize from the look on his face that he was just making idle conversation. My voice trails off.

"Do you remember the MMPI?" he asks. This time I just nod. "It is the Minnesota Multiphasic Personality Inventory," he goes on, as if I hadn't responded. "You took it on the first day you were here." Again I nod, but I don't believe it will make a difference in what he says. "I usually go over it with our clients on the second or third day, but I wanted to wait awhile with you. There are some things I asked the other counselors to confirm in their sessions with you."

His smile catches me off guard. Is there an inside joke here that I am not getting? Is he happy to give me some really good news? Am I about to be surprised to find out there is a pill I can take and make it all go away? I relax my guard a little and lean back on the sofa. I wait for Dr. Dunning to continue and decide the carpet is a couple of years old.

I took the MMPI on the first day I arrived at the clinic. It was several hundred multiple-choice and true-false questions like, "Have you considered robbing a bank?" A-never, B-sometimes, C-often, D-the car is running outside, right now. I remember that it asked the same question many different times, in slightly different forms. It took a couple of hours to finish and I was more confused when I was done, than when I started.

"Tell me something," he says, picking up a manila folder that I can only assume contains the results of my MMPI. "Before we go over this, tell me how you came to The Clinic."

Big silver jet seemed like too snide a comment so I went back as far as the move to Miami and started there.

The move to Miami was wonderful. I was filled with the anticipation of a fresh start and a new challenge. Doris and I had started seeing a counselor in the weeks before we moved. I felt sure that a new place was all we needed. It seemed to me like the counselor, actually counselors, a husband and wife team, had eased some of the tension and stress between Doris and me. They had even brought the boys in and talked to them. It seemed to me that everyone was hopeful and willing to wipe the slate clean.

I was determined that, with this move, the "inappropriate" relationship would be over and I could get back on track. I knew I really did want to be a good husband and father and this move was just what I needed.

As a bonus to that, the church in Miami was a dream-come true. It was a very large, very progressive, very dynamic, international church. Our first Sunday there, we were greeted by hundreds of faces, most of them not white. The congregation was made up of people from more than forty different countries, India to the

West Indies, Germany to Guyana. A large percentage of the people were island people from the Caribbean. They were God-loving, joyful people with a passion for prayer and a zeal for their faith.

The whole church reveled in the Sunday morning worship services with lots of singing, hand clapping, and tambourine playing. They were fun and funny. They loved us and we immediately loved them. We were welcomed with dinners and parties and family reunions. They showered us with cards and small gifts and invitations to supper. Our first few weeks were packed with activity and excitement. We learned to eat *roti* and made whole meals on *arroz con garbanzo*. I was brushing up on my high school Spanish again and starting to work on Haitian Creole.

We found a beautiful little apartment that overlooked the third hole of a world class golf course. The family room of the apartment opened onto a small, screened veranda that we furnished with wicker chairs and giant ferns. There was a ceiling fan with blades that looked like palm fronds. In the evenings we would sit on the veranda and look out over the emerald golf course and act like Harrison had never happened. Doris read Beth Moore. I studied for sermons and Jacob played the guitar. They were good days.

Joshua had graduated from college and bought a house in middle Tennessee. Jacob had graduated from high school and come to live with us. He played bass guitar in the praise band at the church and Doris played the piano. The church began to grow right away and it looked like we had survived a near miss.

Some of the island ladies in the church had a weekly Bible Study. They invited Doris, the single white face in a cluster of brown and black ones. Miss Grace, Sister Rachel, Dortha Mae, they quoted scripture together, sang old hymns *a capella*, and prayed for hours. Doris would come back every week glowing with joy. She also was reading a lot, especially Beth Moore. <u>Breaking Free</u>, <u>When Godly People Do Ungodly Things</u>, and <u>Praying God's Word</u> were mainstays in her diet. I thought it was a good phase she was going through. I had no idea that God was preparing her for the most difficult battle yet. She was growing deeper every day and I wasn't.

I did not understand that a fire burned inside me and, running away, which had worked in the past, was not going to work this time. After all of these years, the addict smoldering inside of me had flamed into a raging inferno in Harrison and it would not be quenched now. I had lost control of myself and my ability to compartmentalize had failed. There was no longer any time that I felt good about myself. I was constantly depressed. I was unable to mask my emotions and what had once been a quiet, small voice now screamed at me constantly, accusing me and reminding me of my shame and guilt and pain. I hurt all the time and craved another "fix." Like any other junkie, I was desperate to medicate away my pain.

Nearly every waking moment there was an all-out war inside me, the man I wanted to be fighting for his life against the horrid beast I thought I was. Every sermon I preached or prayer I prayed was drowned out inside my head by the putrid, pounding recordings of the awful things I had done. And the only way to get relief from the agony of that conflict was to do more awful things. I called the "inappropriate" relationship in Harrison, several times a day. I fantasized about secret meetings and made up excuses to drive back to Harrison. The more the fire burned, the more anti-social and withdrawn I became. I was angry because I had those wrong thoughts and angry because I couldn't act on them. There was no hiding, at least from my family, this terrible inferno that I was doing battle with.

One day when the rage that burned inside of me was blatantly obvious on the outside, Jacob asked Doris, "Is Dad mad at us?" She replied, "Your father is battling an inner demon but God has promised me that he would be healed." In her prayer time God had told her this. A few months later she told me that those promises were what she held on to in the darkest nights.

We had been in Miami only a few months when Easter arrived. I planned a spectacular, international celebration for the church. We had special music, a Spanish choir, African dancers, and radio and television personalities. My sister had come down to be our featured guest artist and, as usual, she packed the house. The weather was gorgeous. We set up a huge tent and on that Easter Sunday, we had the largest crowd in the history of the church. The ushers had purchased matching, gold blazers. The parking lot attendants had on orange vests. The church grounds were immaculate and the congregation was incredible. It was an unbelievable success with hundreds of visitors and a service like nothing any of us had ever seen.

That afternoon Jacob found a phone bill that reflected all of the calls I had made back to Harrison. He was weeping when he showed it to his mother. The next morning, while I was at my office writing letters of praise to all of the people who had worked so hard on Easter Sunday, Doris and Jacob packed the car and left.

Dr. Dunning stops me. To tell the truth, I am so involved in the story that I have almost forgotten he is here. He states more than asks, "That is when you called The Clinic?" I nod. "And that was a month ago, now you are here?" I nod again.

After Doris left, I confessed a part of my story to the leaders of the church in Miami. They wept and hugged me and promised me I could stay and that they would help me find God's healing. We called the state overseer, my friend, and he told me that I was to resign from the church immediately and not go back. That is the rule of the church and I had expected it. So I called a special meeting of the church leaders on a Monday night and quit. They wept. I went home to a dark, empty apartment and sat on the veranda, overlooking the third hole of the golf course, until three o'clock in the morning, then fell asleep on the couch with the television on. For the second time in my adult life I had no job, no home, no career, and no future. And now, I had no family.

When the sun came up I tried to read but the words on the page were lifeless and meaningless. I could not concentrate on two consecutive sentences much less get something coherent from a book. I paced the apartment and wept. I buried my face in a pillow and screamed. I watched the clock tick seconds that seemed like hours until it was a reasonable time and then I called the counselors that we had seen in Harrison. They listened quietly to my telephone ranting. I really have no idea what I said. I know I begged for help and told them I was willing to do anything to get my family back. At the end of the conversation, they gave me the phone number of The Clinic.

We had just sold our house in Harrison and the money we cleared was enough to pay the tuition at The Clinic for a few weeks, buy a round trip ticket, and book a cheap motel a couple of miles away. The first opening was three weeks away but I scheduled everything that morning anyway. By eleven o'clock I had done all that I knew to do and I sat down and waited for my life to disintegrate. I thought back over every lie I had told, every sin I had committed, every trust I had betrayed. I imagined the pain I had caused my wife and my sons. I reflected on the shame I had brought on the church. I watched the hands on the clock tick the seconds away. I picked up the phone and put it back down a thousand times. I didn't know who to call. When it got dark, I sat on the veranda for the second straight night until three o'clock in the morning, then moved to the couch again and wondered if the sun would ever come up again.

Dr. Dunning stands up and I think our session must be over. Instead, he comes around the desk and sits on a sofa across from me. He opens the manila folder in his hands without looking at it. He is looking intently at me, sizing me up, I think, deciding how much I can bear. He states again, "You took the Minnesota Mutiphasic Personality Inventory the first day you arrived. It gives us a very accurate picture of who you are and what we are dealing with." I wonder to myself who the "we" is that he refers to. Does he mean the counselors and the staff? He and I? Who is dealing with this creature he is about to describe from this mysterious Minnesota Multiphasic Personality Inventory?

With that, he begins to read from the folder in his hand, not making eye contact, no emotion. He reads in a monotone without looking up. I have never been in the cockpit of a passenger jet during the preflight checklist but, I imagine they use the same kind of businesslike, no-nonsense voice. "Fuel. Check. Wings. Check. Tires. Check." One by one he goes down an invisible list and checks off the most horrid personality traits I could imagine.

"You are a liar, almost pathological. You seem unable to tell the truth, especially to yourself, and you lie about almost everything. In some cases you have lied for so long that you may not even know what the truth is."

I catch my breath to protest but he doesn't even look up.

"You are a predator. You use your position and influence to prey on weak and vulnerable women. You are constantly sizing them up and preparing them for your attack. You use people to meet and satisfy your own cravings and then, you leave them discarded behind you."

My face is burning with anger and shame. I interrupt him, "That is not true. I am not a predator."

He looks at me as if I am speaking a foreign language that he does not understand. He waves the folder in front of me like a matador's cape and says, "This is not my opinion. This is what your inventory and your history says. You may not like it. You may not want to accept it, but this is who you are."

That settled, he goes back to the folder. "It says here that you have a personality disorder. Your addiction to lust, and to being loved, has taken from you the ability to control your actions. You are powerless over your desires and, what you have done in the past, you will do in the future, over and over again.

"You are an adulterer. You are a thief. You are a cheat. You have stolen joy and happiness from your wife, your children and countless other families. You have destroyed lives and ruined churches. You have taken what you wanted, regardless of the cost to others, and focused all of your efforts on pleasing yourself.

"You have nearly destroyed your wife and your sons. You have broken their hearts and scarred them. You have made them suffer so that you can be gratified."

By now I am sobbing uncontrollably. I feel as if my heart has exploded inside my chest. I can't catch my breath. My ears are ringing; I hear him, but it is as though he is speaking through a glass wall. I am literally unable to raise my head, or make eye contact. I hear other words being uttered and then realize they are mine. I am repeating only one phrase and that, over and over again. "I don't want to be this way. I don't want to be this way." Obviously, inherent in this cry is my acknowledgement that all Dr. Dunning is saying is true. I can only respond, "I don't want to be this way. I don't want to be this way."

Dr. Dunning tells the truth. He is incapable of anything less than absolute truth. He stands and offers me a wad of Kleenex, then walks to the door, signifying it is time for me to leave. As I stumble out of his office, his only comment is, "I'm sure you don't. No one would want to be this way."

I find my way back to the waiting room and take my usual seat in the corner. It is crowded and hot, with a steady drone of hushed conversations. By now I know that people in the waiting room do not pay attention when a "basketcase" comes stumbling out of a session and drips tears of anguish all over the floor. But even if they did, it would not matter. I am oblivious to anything else. My mind is racing through the pre-crash checklist. "Liar. Check. Predator. Check. Adulterer. Check. Personality Disorder. Check."

Chapter 11

DARK

It is the genius of The Clinic, or the grace of God, that has me scheduled with Kay Heinz for my last session of the day. I am not sure which, but I know that if any other therapist was on the sheet, I would leave The Clinic for good. I am on the verge of doing that anyway. I cannot remember a time when I felt more devastated, more alone, more in despair, than this moment. I am sure all of the things Dr. Dunning just told me are true. I am also sure that I probably knew most of them, deep, down, somewhere in the dark corners of my soul, places that I kept isolated and compartmentalized from everyday cognizance. But, the weight of hearing everything, all at once, laid out like a stinking, gutted pig on the slaughter house floor, is more than I can stand. I am at the "bottom."

I am trying to clear my mind enough to decide when to leave and where to go when Kay Heinz comes to the waiting room door and calls my name. I have had several sessions with her already and she is the nurse of mercy in this hospital of hopelessness. She is tall, over six feet, and graceful, a woman in her early forties, I guess. Her facial expression easily shifts from a gentle, knowing smile to a tender look of concern. Her voice is soft, soothing and dripping with empathy and care. In another setting she might be too sweet to be real but here, after hours of brutal, straightforward confrontation, she is the sugar that makes lemonade palatable.

She is the perfect comforter. By the grace of God, I need her at this moment.

Her office is in the building across the street, down the hall from Dr. Rivers. We walk across the parking lot, in the late afternoon sunlight, in silence. She must sense that idle chat about the weather would put me over the edge. My eyes are swollen and I squint against the still blazing, late afternoon, Arizona sky. I follow Dr. Heinz numbly. I don't know what else to do.

As we settle into her office, she asks immediately, "How are you?" Her office is small and dainty. Pictures of her family are arranged by age on a little bookshelf in the corner. Her desk is really a small sewing table, an antique handed down from her grandmother, I imagine. She never sits behind it but always off to one side in an uncomfortable-looking Queen Anne kind of chair with flowery print upholstery. I sit on an equally flowery love seat and face a wall that is decorated with a crocheted rendition of the Madonna and Child.

Dr. Heinz asks softly again, "How are you?" It creates the tiny crack that is all the dam needs to explode from the pent up pressure behind it. I sob, nearly hysterical, and try to describe the MMPI session with Dr. Dunning. I am angry and embarrassed and ashamed all at once. I try to regain my composure in front of this kind, attractive woman, but the emotions are too powerful and, for what seems like an hour, I gush despair, depression, and dismay all over her flowery carpet. I am defeated. I have come to the absolute end of my psychological rope. Where before I thought I had experienced depression, now I know what abject hopelessness and despondency feels like. I am destroyed.

She listens patiently, sometimes with a knowing smile and sometimes with an empathetic look of concern. I realize that she must be fully aware of the content of my folder. The staff of therapists surely discuss it thoroughly at Evaluation. I also realize that she is not going to contradict what Dr. Dunning has said. To be honest, I am not asking for that. For one of the first times, I do not want to feel better. I want to get well or die and, right now, to die seems like the better choice. Kay is just here to guide me through the pain. I feel like a hospice patient listening to my caregiver say, "There is nothing we can do to heal you. We will try to make you more comfortable in your final hours."

Ashi did that for me in Miami.

Ashi invited me to play tennis shortly after we moved to Miami. He was a big man, an Indian businessman. Not a wild-west Indian but an India Indian. For his size, he had cat-like reflexes on the tennis court and a lion-like heart for God, and for people. He became my dearest friend almost at once, and our twice-a-week tennis matches became moments of genuine grace for me.

We would meet early in the morning to beat the Florida heat, usually Tuesday and Friday. We would warm up for a few minutes, Ashi pounding the ball at me while I scrambled in utter self-defense. And then we would take a break and pray. Ashi was one of those rare men who seemed able to exude strength and mascu-linity and at the same time be so tender before God. I loved to hear him pray. He would pray there on the side of the tennis court in his heavy, Indian accent, for my family, for my ministry, for my heart. He never raised his voice or forced his prayer but I always felt, when He prayed, that God stopped whatever He was doing and turned His face toward Ashi, careful not to miss a word. Ashi was a man of God and he was my friend.

He came from a missionary family of noble proportions. His father had been a missionary from India to the United States, the leader of many great churches. His brother was a respected, well-known, theologian and seminary professor. Ashi built a small business empire by working hard, using his God-given savvy and having a reputation of impeccable integrity. His business, like his family, and his life, was completely dedicated to God and everything that he did, reflected that idea. There was an aura of God-centeredness about him that was not at all uncomfortable or out of place. It seemed the most natural thing in the world to hear him tell the tennis score, "Forty-love, praise God."

He was one of the leaders of the church at Miami on the Monday night that I told them Doris had left. The next morning he called me and said, "Pastor, let's go play tennis." Two or three times a week, in the month that followed, Ashi took me to the tennis court and prayed with me. He neither condemned nor condoned. He did not offer advice or make suggestions about what I should do to get my family back. If I talked, he listened. If I was silent, we played tennis. But always, he prayed. I am sure that I survived those dark and painful days only by the grace of God and the prayers and friendship of Ashi.

Dr. Heinz listens to all of this with a knowing smile and then asks softly, "Is Ashi still your friend?" I nod in the affirmative and then she asks, "And does God still offer grace?" I am too broken to respond. I don't know. This is the question that haunts me the most. "Where is God in all of this? If He made me, did He make me flawed? Did He not listen when I begged him to change me? Where is His grace for me?" In fact, l feel like everything that I have heard today only confirms what I have known all along: God does not love me. He created me in the dark and has left me there my whole life, in spite of all my efforts.

Her tender look of concern is replaced by a knowing smile and Dr. Heinz gives me an assignment. "I want you to write a letter to God," she says. "I want you to be completely honest and not pull any punches. Tell Him exactly how you feel about all that you have heard today and all that you have been through in your life. Write it all out and bring in to me in the morning." She puts her hand under my chin and raises my face, forcing me to look her in the eyes. "Mike, do you promise me you will bring it to me in the morning?"

I like Dr. Heinz. She has been a "friend" when the other counselors were so confrontational that I couldn't stand it any longer. I promise her I will bring it in the morning. She stands to signify our session is over but before I leave she prays for me. I get the feeling that God stops what He is doing and turns His face toward Kay Heinz so as not to miss a word.

Chapter 12

THE LETTER

The motel where I am staying in Scottsdale is a cheap, seedy sort of place about two miles from The Clinic. It is one of those motels with a number in the name--Motel Six, Super Eight--anything like that can't be very nice. But with the expense of treatment and the flight from Miami, it is all that I can afford. A rental car is not in the budget either, so I walk to The Clinic every morning about six and walk back every night about ten . Even at those times in Arizona, the heat sweeps up from the pavement and slaps me in the face.

Tonight I don't notice it, or at least don't care. The small amount of comfort I received from Kay Heinz has faded and my mind is back to ruminating over the session with Dr. Dunning. I have been weeping for what seems like hours now. It is not the healing kind of crying that brings relief. Instead every sob drives me to a darker, more frightening place. I am trying to rationally think through all that I have felt and heard, trying to get some sort of game plan together, but nothing comes. There is a black, impenetrable curtain that prevents me from thinking at all. All I can do is remember.

"You have destroyed your wife and family," I hear him say. "You have damaged the church and ruined lives. You cannot change. You have a personality disorder." I don't know why, but that phrase, personality disorder, is the most devastating of all to me. It sounds like something along the line of "inoperable" or "terminal illness." It screams of hopelessness. I am out of options.

Options. As I walk, I weigh them. What can I do to release my family from the torment I have created for them? How can I go on living with the certainty that I am a flawed person? For maybe the first time ever, I very seriously begin to consider suicide. I think through a number of possible methods, carefully comparing each, measuring pros and cons, like a teenager shopping for a used car. Deep in my heart, I know that my fear of God is too great, and the terror of an eternal consequence brings me to conclude that there is no solution in suicide. Is that in itself an act of grace? Is God trying to deliver me from myself? I am still too removed from Him to give those thoughts much credence.

But still, my family and the pain I have caused, haunts me. I turn my cell phone on. I keep it off during the day to preserve the battery and to avoid any contact with the "inappropriate relationship." I dial my wife's number and leave the only message that makes sense to me at the moment. It is as sincere and as heartfelt as I have ever been. I believe it is the only reasonable solution and in the fog of my emotional duress I feel like it will remedy the catastrophic situation, at least for Doris and the boys. "I am not coming back," I sob into the phone. She is asleep, I know, and her phone will be turned off. I talk to her voicemail with every ounce of passion in me. I hope somehow that the depth of my feeling will come through and she will understand that this is the only way out for us. "I am not coming back. In the morning I will disappear--California, Mexico, wherever a bus ticket will take me. Get a divorce. Go on with your life. Tell the boys that I love them, that I am so sorry, I do not want to be this way." If I know my heart, there is no self-pity in this message, no attempt to manipulate. It makes perfect sense to me and it is all that I have left to do. "I love you," I say to the voicemail. "I always have. I hope that you can believe that."

I have walked from the clinic to the motel so often that I can do it without thinking. There are a couple of different routes but all take about the same amount of time, fifty minutes. Tonight

I wander long, out of the way blocks. I turn up and down dark streets, never getting too far from the motel but unwilling to go back to the room. I have turned my phone off again, trying to preserve the battery and also, because I am so spent that I cannot take another single, emotional input. I have no desire to eat. I know I cannot sleep. I cannot focus or concentrate on a book or television program. I know of nothing else to do but walk, and so, I walk. Sometimes I circle the same block three or four times. Sometimes I simply turn around and retrace my steps.

Finally, about two AM, I turn the key in the door of my second floor motel room and step inside without turning on the light. I lay down on the bed not bothering to pull down the covers or take off my clothes. I just lay there, looking up at a ceiling that I cannot see and listening to the streets sounds from outside. My mind races, careening from thought to thought, nothing coherent, nothing focused. I try to think about what to do next, where to go from here, but nothing comes.

Suddenly I remember the letter and the promise I made to Dr. Heinz. It seems like the only kind of action I can come up with so I get up, turn on the light, and begin to write.

"Dear God,
I am afraid of you. I am afraid to write this letter and tell you what I really feel. I know that you know, but somehow, until I actually articulate it, I'm not really guilty of the sacrilege and heresy that this letter, and my heart, may contain. It seems I am so messed up and flawed that I am pretty much damned anyway. I am damned if I write it and damned if I don't. It can't get much worse and, who knows, maybe it will help.

Why did you do this to me? Why did you play this horrible, cruel joke and torment me the way you have? Who am I that you would choose to create me in a way that I would live in conflict and chaos, inside and out? Tell me, if you will, what I ever did to deserve the agony of such a flawed personality?

I am made in your image. But how did you allow that image to become so distorted that it reflects nearly the opposite of what it desires to be? Did you make a mistake? Were you not strong enough to protect me? Did you just forget that I am here? Or worst of all, am I some cosmic experiment, a trial-and-error project that turned out wrong?

You tell me to love you. You even put in my heart a desperate desire to do so. Then you create a cold, calculating muscle in me that pumps blood but cannot open itself up beyond that. I pray so often for you to remove my heart of stone and give me a heart of flesh. Each prayer is met with silence, or worse, condemnation.

You call me to a life of purity. You place me in a community that lauds holiness and holy living. And then you twist my character and pervert my desires. You increase my pain and present me with shameful analgesics. Wrong, horrifically wrong acts become my comfort and my curse. I fail to be holy and the agony of that drives me to hedonism. And hedonism tears me to shreds because it is so far from the holy I desire to be. Are you toying with me?

You challenge me to surrender, to let go and let God. You surround me with simple epithets and sincere people that say put everything in God's hands. And then you create in me a controlling spirit, a manipulative manner. You tell me to release it all and then make it impossible for me to do so. And when I have, in all honesty, you have failed me more often than not.

- I prayed for my dad. He disappeared.
- I prayed for my sister, Charlotta. You broke her neck.
- I prayed for my sister, Cheralyn. You gave her cancer.
- I prayed for deliverance. It did not come.
- I prayed for mercy. It doesn't happen.
- I prayed to die. I'm still here.

Tell me how to trust you. Show me a way to get beyond all of that and find a faith that is personal.

Do I believe in you? Absolutely. Do I think you are good and have a sincere interest in mankind? Without a doubt. Am I convinced of your omnipotence and your omnipresence? Surely I am. But when it comes to me, Mike Courtney, this single, solitary piece of garbage, you have chosen to be absent at least, and even, antagonistic at times.

'But what about free will?' someone might ask. 'We are free moral agents you know. We all bear responsibility for our actions.' That is baloney. I am not talking about simply making choices. I have made terrible ones and I own up to them. I am talking about a moral makeup, a personal, private penchant for sorrow and isolation and despair, placed in me by the Creator of the universe.

<u>That</u> you could change. <u>That</u> you could have prevented, or corrected, or cured. Have I allowed that personality flaw to cause me to scar myself and others with sin and sickness? Yes. And for that I am deeply and sincerely sorry. I, and I alone, am to blame for my actions. And I will take my punishment and do my work.

But to be created this way, to be made defective, damaged from the beginning and discarded early on, that is your doing. You, O God, are responsible. You made me in my mother's womb. You ordered my days before one of them came to be. Why? I only ask why?

And I beg you one more time to take this lot from me. It is more than I can bear. If it is a test, I have failed it. So please remove this agony, stop the hurt and the hurting that I do. Cure me or kill me but get me out of this despair. I can't go on.

I am afraid of you. I am afraid to write this letter. But I am more afraid of staying the same, of finishing out my days no better than the bulk of my life has been. And so I write, and I pray and I plead. I am powerless, O Lord, doomed to failure and futility unless you intervene.

Let me love you. Let me open my closed heart and know that I love you. Maybe more important, <u>let me know that you love me</u>. Keep me pure. Deliver me from evil. Help me to do the things I want to do and resist the things I don't. And teach me to release, surrender, give up, let go. I don't know what else to do. I don't know where else to turn. To whom shall I go? You have the words of eternal life. I still believe that."

It is after three AM when I finish writing. I turn off the light and lay back down, without pulling back the cover or taking off my clothes. I have fulfilled half of my promise to Kay Heinz. After a few hours of sleep I will fulfill the other half. I will take the letter to her, and then I will leave. I have enough money for a bus ticket to Mexico. There I will disappear and end the cycle of hurt and shame that I have brought on everyone I have touched.

I have destroyed my wife and sons. I have damaged the church. I have ruined the lives of others. And now I am sure I have done the final, despicable, unthinkable act. I have cursed God so that He will never, ever turn His face toward me again. Tonight is the last night of my life as I know it. Tomorrow…I am drifting into a fitful sleep…everything will change tomorrow.

Chapter 13

DORTHA MAE

I am jolted awake by the cheap alarm clock that has gone off at five-fifteen every morning since I arrived. For a few seconds it feels like a bad dream, all of it, but only for a few seconds. Almost before my eyes are open, the incredible heaviness of the day before sweeps over me. I shower and shave like a man facing the electric chair. There is no satisfaction of having made a decision, no relief in knowing that by the end of the day it will all be over. I am a "dead man walking," a condemned prisoner going through the motions of a last meal and a visit by the priest.

I pick up my letter and close the door behind me. The sun is bright, as usual in the early desert morning, and it is hot already. Dry heat is not all it's cracked up to be. One-hundred-and-twelve is still hot, whether dry or wet. This morning it must be in the high seventies or low eighties already. I pass a bank with the temperature posted on the sign on my way. I make a mental note to check the temperature when I walk by.

It is interesting to me how the mind can gravitate to the mundane in the middle of the most distressing of times. During the days after the girls died, I remember how much talk went into what to prepare for the Southern "after the funeral meals." When my father left, I remember spending a lot of mental effort arranging the wrenches on the peg board in his garage. When I was having affairs in Swansea and in Harrison, I would sit for hours and calculate Sunday School averages and offering records. There is an escape, I guess, in worrying about the temperature or planning a menu when your life is falling apart.

I have promised Dr. Heinz that I will come back this morning and deliver to her the letter I wrote to God. It is the only reason I can think of to return to The Clinic one more day. The treatment will not work, Dr. Dunning as much as said so. I cannot change. The sooner I disappear, the better for my family. My father dropped out of sight for a half-dozen years. I had no contact with him, no idea where he was. I survived, so will Josh and Jacob.

That thought is all that it takes for the tears to begin to stream again. My eyes are cloudy and seeing is difficult because of the flow, but I have made this walk so many times that I just keep putting one foot in front of the other.

I pass the bank and the sign says seventy-eight degrees at six-twelve AM. The next screen flashes the date. It is the sixth of June. Father's Day is next weekend.

My sons, Joshua and Jacob are remarkable young men. They both exhibit a maturity always that is far beyond what I showed at their age. Joshua is so like his mother, a gentle but remarkably strong spirit, with a depth of compassion for people that is amazing. Jacob takes after me, at least the good stuff in me. He is outgoing and gregarious, the life of every party, but he has a passion for God and an eye for the underdog.

During the lonely days in Miami, after Doris and Jacob left, I tried to journal. Much of what I wrote, I wrote to my sons. I didn't know if they would ever read it. I didn't know if they would ever speak to me again. They were both hurt so deeply and angry at the lies and at the pain I had caused their mother. Doris told me that Joshua refused to talk to me, or even about me. When she tried to pray for me, he would leave the room. He was so broken by what I had done that he could not eat or sleep.

Jacob, on the other hand wanted to come back to Miami, so that I would not be alone. He told his mother that he would come back and stay at the apartment with me until I could get back on my feet. He was barely out of high school, in fact an early graduate, and already a rescuer. I prayed every day during that time that God would deliver them from the generational curse that had defeated me.

My reverie is broken as I cross the last street before The Clinic. There is a concrete bench, a bus stop, I think, that I sit on every morning and wait for the secretary to unlock the doors. Today I decide to turn on my cell phone and listen to any messages that might have come. I wait for the phone to engage and finally hear the words, "You have one message." I push the button to play the message. It is from Dortha Mae.

Doris began attending a Women's Bible Study while we were in Miami. Island ladies who sang with gusto, though a little off key, and loved God vigorously. They trusted Him implicitly and Doris was blessed by every encounter she had with them. One of the main ladies in the group was Dortha Mae.

Dortha Mae is a dignified, and very dark, woman from Barbados. Her story is the stuff that books were written about. She had escaped the poverty of her island as a teenage girl by hiring on as a maid on a ship bound for London. She worked for years in England as a chamber maid for the very rich and then, as a seamstress, making the fine ballroom gowns that noble ladies required for their lives of fashion.

Dortha married in England, and she and her husband moved to Canada to work in the garment industry of Toronto and Montreal. There, she found two things, a gift for designing and a heart for God. In a little street mission in Toronto, Dortha Mae gave her life to Jesus, really. She became a follower of Christ with a fervor that overwhelmed most, including her husband. He left her in Toronto with a young family and no money.

She moved her family to New York City, and before long, became one of the leading designers of expensive women's clothes. Rich ladies would come from all over the world to have Dortha Mae design and make a dress for them. I imagined the beauty and grace of her inner life were somehow woven into the fabric of her creations. God blessed Dortha Mae and she was faithful to Him.

By the time we came to know her in Miami, all of that was behind her. She was a retired, single lady living in a small duplex, not far from the church. Her children had grown and gone on to become successful business owners in other parts of the country. Dortha Mae was left alone with her Bible Study, and with God. That seemed to be enough. She was passionate about church, about God, and about life.

She never learned to drive so I would pick her up for Sunday service. She would greet me each Sunday with a huge smile and a genuine joy that was infectious. "Pastor," she would say in a thick, island accent, "This is the day the Lord has made. Let us REJOICE and be glad in it." When Dortha Mae said "REJOICE," she did.

She loved to sing in the choir. What Dortha Mae lacked in vocal quality she more than made up for in quantity. She had a booming alto voice that could not, and would not ,be hidden. Our choir was made up of sopranos, tenors, basses, altos and Dortha Mae. No matter what the song or what the style, Dortha Mae threw back her head and belted out the music in a way that made everyone in the congregation smile. She could not sing without her feet moving. She sang and danced and we smiled and laughed.

I am surprised that the phone message is from Dortha Mae. I listen there, on the side of the street, in Scottsdale, Arizona, to this lady from Barbados, calling from Miami, and giving me a message, straight from heaven. "Pastor," she says with authority, "This is the day the Lord has made. I will REJOICE and be glad in it." I begin to weep again as I think back over my Sunday mornings with Dortha Mae. "I am praying for you and for Sister Doris," she continues. "And God has given me this Word. You will not be defeated. You will not be destroyed. God has said 'I will repay you for the years that the locusts have eaten. You will praise the name of the Lord your God who has worked wonders for you.' God is not finished with you, Pastor. He loves you and you will be healed."

I am blinded by the tears. I listen to the message over and over again until the battery in my phone begins to fade. I listen with hope, with dismay, with gladness, with sadness. I listen to Dortha Mae, wanting desperately to believe that what she says is true and at the same time, distraught at the reminder of all that I have lost. But I keep listening, and in the voice of that beautiful, black woman I find the strength to walk across the street and enter The Clinic for one more day.

Chapter 14

VISION

Each morning at The Clinic, the "inmates" arrive in the waiting room and pick up their counseling schedule for the day. By now, we know one another, and the counselors, well enough to compare notes and have fun. "Oh no, I've got Rivers right before lunch." "You'll be late. He always goes over." "Man, Carlson at two o'clock." "Boring. Expect a good nap." We are like college freshmen signing up for classes. Funny except for the fact that we are all men and women whose lives are crumbling while we sit in here and make jokes about our therapists.

I don't feel much like joking today. I quickly, and quietly, pick up my schedule and go to my usual spot in the corner to wait for therapy to begin. My first session is with Andie Bowman, then Group. Kay Heinz is the third session of the day. I don't look beyond that. At this point, I plan to deliver my letter and leave. I have fought this thing long enough. I am not blaming anyone, especially God, but there appears to be no respite from the terrible lot that has been handed me. This desperate feeling of unlovability, and the destructive search for love has brought me to the end of my rope. I don't have the courage to take my life but, I can at least take my disease somewhere else, where the people that I care about will be safe from me. I know how Adam felt in the Garden of Eden. Even though I know it is impossible, I am trying to hide from God.

As I sit and wait on this day, one of the "inmates," a pock-faced old man named Frank, sits down beside me. We have learned quite a few things about each other in group, but a last name is not one of them. I know how old he is. I know where he comes from. I know what he did for a living, and I know about his offenses, who he touched, and the addiction that brought him to this place. He knows my name is Mike, little else.

He is a nasty man, not the kind of person I would have spent time with on the outside. He has the appearance of an offender. Years of addiction and secrecy have left him furtive looking. He seems to look over me, or behind me, as we talk. His hands never stop moving, picking invisible lint from his wrinkled slacks, or searching his breast pocket for a pen that isn't there. His teeth are yellowed and his skin is scaly. He sits too close and talks too loud. But he has a message that he seems to think I should hear.

"I was praying today and God gave me a verse for you," he says. To my surprise he pulls out a faded old Bible that is well used and heavily marked. "Zephaniah 3:17," Frank blurts, "'The Lord your God is with you, He is mighty to save. He will take great delight in you, He will quiet you with His love, **He will rejoice over you with singing.'**"

Tears are pouring from my eyes so that the waiting room takes on an almost heavenly shimmer, and Frank looks like, well, like an angel. He leans even closer and he whispers like a little kid who has discovered what he is getting for Christmas, "Can you believe, the God who created the universe, knelt down beside your bed this morning and sang over you?"

I wrote God the letter last night. I know He knows every angry, sacrilegious word I said. And while I was lying on top of the covers in a seedy motel room in Scottsdale, with the letter folded on the night-stand, God knelt beside my bed this morning and sang over me. I need so to believe that it is true. Like a thirst-crazed man, stranded in the Arizona desert, my empty, broken spirit is gasping for every drop of hope that I can imagine in Frank's words. With tears soaking my face, I lean over and grab Frank around the neck. I hug him as tightly as I have ever hugged any person in my life.

Not something you want to do in a clinic full of perverts and sex addicts. I don't care. First Dortha Mae and now Frank, I was hoping for hope and they are telling me it is here.

If only I could know. If only I could feel something to make me sure that everything I had been preaching and teaching and believing for others was true in my life. God loves me? He delights in me? Isn't there someway I can be sure?

I am not sure what Andie Bowman thinks when she opens the door and sees me locked in an embrace with Frank. I am too broken to care. I follow her back to the bright office full of over-stuffed pillows. She motions for me to sit in a straight-backed chair that she has placed in the middle of the room and then begins to tell me about a new kind of therapy called EMDR.

"Eye Movement Desensitizing and Reprocessing is a tool that interrupts your stream of consciousness and allows you to bring up some deep thoughts and feelings that might otherwise be hard to get to," explains Dr. Bowman. "We don't know for sure how it works," she continues, "Dr. Rivers calls it voodoo." As she talks, Dr. Bowman is unpacking a small, but strange-looking machine that is about the size of a laptop computer. It has a digital light bar built into the lid, like a miniature bank sign that tells time and temperature. I wonder if this will do the same. There are a series of dials across the face and a place to plug in headphones, which Dr. Bowman does. The most ominous looking parts of the contraption are two wires extending, one from each side, attached to little metal plates, about the size of silver dollars.

Dr. Bowman talks as she sits the voodoo machine on a table in front of me. "The purpose is to change your normal thinking patterns," she says. "You will see different colored lights flash on the screen. The headphones will play alternating beeps in your ears. And when you hold the discs, they will pulsate back and forth. Like the rapid eye movement in sleep, these sensory impulses will bring you to a dream-like state of open consciousness."

She places the headphones on my head and I just nod. I am thinking I will not have to escape to Mexico. I am going to be electrocuted right here among the overstuffed pillows. I start to wonder just what those pillows are stuffed with. Maybe they contain the bodies of all of the patients before me that have succumbed to the dreaded EMDR voodoo machine.

She asks, "What are you feeling this morning?" The little bit of amusement I have found in her preparation evaporates and I am flooded, again, with the agony and despair that began yesterday afternoon. I explain that to her, and she moves over to stand beside the machine. "Have you ever felt anything close to this despair before?"

After the first affair, in Midland, Doris was distant and withdrawn for a long time. I tried to make up for my offense by being attentive and affectionate but my attempts were rejected. One afternoon, several weeks after the affair, she responded to my advances and we were intimate. After, as I lay beside her on the couch, my hand brushed her cheek and I felt that it was wet with tears. It is a memory too painful for words, an agonizing moment of shame and sorrow, when the hurt I felt was dwarfed by the hurt that I had caused. My own tears scalded my face. I felt a tightness in my chest, and a burning rock in my gut that made it impossible to breathe.

Zap. Zap. Dr. Bowman hits me with a pulsating attack on my senses that interrupt, not only the story I am telling her, but my train of thought. There is a low frequency beeping in the headphones, moving from one side to the other. The light panel is flashing a red and blue--Morse Code--kind of signal. The discs, that I hold in my hands, vibrate, alternating from one hand to the other in something akin to the tingle you feel when you touch the spark plug of a lawnmower. "Now what do you see?" she asks.

Inexplicably, I see a picture that sat on my desk for years. It was one of my favorites. Joshua is lounging on a huge, driftwood relic on the beach at Sanibel Island in Florida. He is a tousle-headed, three year old, squinting against the glare of bright sun on white sand. His skin is perfect, unblemished and unmarked. His face is angelic, without a flaw except for the single, absent tooth in the middle of his smile that makes him look even more perfect. It is a photographic guarantee that there had been idyllic days. We had rented bikes, Doris and I, with a seat for Joshua, and ridden to an old lighthouse on the island. On the way back we stopped at an ice cream parlor, complete with red-and-white striped table clothes, and then, here on the beach, to pick up sea shells and take pictures.

Zap. Zap. More beeps and blinks and the same question: "Now what do you see?"

The vision changes. It is obvious that my thoughts are random, not following a chronological pattern. I see Joshua again, the day he was born.

Doris and I had not been in Midland long. I missed a softball game and we went to the hospital. He was born at seven-twelve PM on May the fifth. There was a "minor" complication and he wasn't breathing well. The nurse very quickly, and without panic, took him from Doris and put him in a tiny, oxygen-enriched incubator. I would not have known anything was out of the ordinary were it not for the doctor, a friend of ours, explaining things to us. Within a matter of minutes, maybe five, his color changed from a faint gray to bright purple and red. And he began to scream. All good things the doctor assured us. They must have been good because the nurse took him out of the incubator and placed Joshua in my arms. At that moment all of the love and compassion that one human being could possibly feel for another, welled up in me as I looked down into the face of my son.

Zap. Zap. Beep. Beep. The pulse begins again and the vision changes. This time I see something not from my memory bank, but from somewhere else. Joshua and Jacob are standing side by side, two tall, strong handsome adult men. They are in their early and mid-forties, I think. They are bookends, bronze statues, monuments to manhood and masculinity. I recognize immediately, somehow, that they are successful and content, men of the world, respected and loved, with great hearts for God. They stand, in my vision, on either side of a slightly bent, wrinkled old man. His hair is thinning and white. His eyes are just beginning to take on the sunken hollowness of old age, but, somehow I know, that this old man is happy, at peace with himself and with God, and with these men that stand beside him. I recognize in my vision that the old man is me. And I understand intuitively that all three men exude respect and affection for one another. All is right in their world.

Zap. Zap. The voodoo machine comes to life again and I am startled from this picture that I do not want to leave. Tears are flowing, but not tears of despair. Instead, for the first time in weeks, certainly for the first time since my meeting with Dr. Dunning yesterday, I am crying tears of hope. After all of the sin and shame, after years of failing and falling, is it thinkable that I may be forgiven? Is peace possible? Could I someday, somehow, feel genuinely loved, even by two of the people that I have wounded most deeply? I hope so. God, I hope so.

A voice speaks out of nowhere. It is Dr. Bowman. "Tell me what you see now," she says. And I tell her, I surprise myself, even as I say it, "I see God."

I am the same stoop-shouldered, white-haired, old man that I saw just a moment ago. I know at once that I am dead, but there is no fear, no sorrow, no remorse. I am in heaven. I don't know how I know that, I just know. I see no features around me, no streets of gold, or mansions over the hilltop. I am not walking on the clouds or floating in space. In fact, the geography and topography of the place are so unimportant as to be invisible in my vision. The only thing that has any consequence is the figure that stands before me. It is God, of this I am quite sure. He is big and powerful, but not at all intimidating. He stands in a colorless tunic as if nothing, even color can be allowed to distract from Him. He is ancient, not old, not elderly, just timeless. Ancient. I can identify nothing of his face except to say there is a radiance. It is not blinding. I don't squint or strain against it. Again, there is no kind of discomfort at all. But the radiance is all that I can distinguish of facial features. I would say He is beaming. Implicit in that thought is a smile.

In my vision, I take a step toward God but He, without rush or hurry, without even movement, covers the distance between us until we stand face to face. There is such a serenity and calm that I feel like I am right where I have always longed to be, safe, and welcome.

God opens His arms wide, inviting me to step into His embrace. His tunic flows without wrinkle or sound. The radiant glow envelopes, not just His face, but His whole being. He speaks to me in a voice that is booming but not loud, full of authority but not authoritative. I am not afraid. There is no doubt in me. I am completely at ease and God says, **"I love you. I have <u>always</u> loved you."**

As I describe this scene to Dr. Bowman I am overwhelmed. I literally fall to one side and sob into one of the overstuffed pillows on the sofa bedside me. I sob and sob and sob in great waves of emotional release. At that moment, in that instant, it is as if everything from the past and the present, every negative anything is swept away. All of the shame and hurt, feelings of abandonment and unworthiness, fear of the future and regret for failures, everything is absolutely, completely erased. There is a cleansing and a wholeness that comes over me that is simply indescribable. In that instant, I know beyond a shadow of a doubt what I have longed to know my whole life. I know that I am loved. In one, all-encompassing epiphany, I am certain that God loves me, and not only God, but my sons, my wife, my friends, my family. All of those people who down through the years have tried to love me, in spite of myself, they really did.

Right then and there I am engulfed in a tsunami of knowing. It does not happen step by step but all at once. It washes over me, I am not unlovable. I have been and am loved. I know that my actions have damaged that love in some. I know that my sons will have to be allowed to process, grieve and forgive. I know that my wonderful wife, whose love I have rejected time and again, may never be able to love me again. I know that there are people that I have hurt that will hold it against me until the day I stand before God, the day I just witnessed. But none of that diminishes the fact that God loves me. He always has. And if He does, then others have, and, perhaps, will love me again.

Finally I regain my composure and sit upright. The sobbing ceases. My tears stop. Dr. Bowman removes the headphones, takes the silver discs from my hands, and turns off the voodoo machine. I know that our session is over. I know that I have more sessions that day. I know that I have more work, lots of work, in the days ahead to rebuild my broken life. But as I stand, faint and weak-kneed, I know two more things: I am a person who is loved, and, in this moment, on this couch surrounded by overstuffed pillows and strapped to a "voodoo machine," I have hope!

There is a movie that I love, *The Legend of Bagger Vance*. Rannulph Junuh is a world class golfer that has lost his 'authentic swing' in the trauma and tragedy of war. He finds himself trying to find himself in an exhibition golf match with Bobby Jones and Walter Hagen. Will Smith plays the mystical caddy, Bagger Vance, and at one crucial point, when Junnuh is about to quit and go back to the despair from which he came, Bagger Vance says this, "Ain't a soul on this entire earth ain't got a burden to carry that he don't understand. You been carrying this one long enough. It's time for you to go on and lay it down. It's time for you to come on out the shadows, Junnuh. It's time for you to choose."

Somehow, in the miracle of this moment, on an overstuffed couch, hooked to a contraption that no one understands, I have laid my burden down. I know that when I step out of this office, I am stepping out of the shadows. If God loves me, then so do others. I know this.

One more thing Bagger Vance says at the end of that scene: "You ain't in this alone. I'm right here with you. I been here all along." This morning, in the midst of zips and zaps, in Andie Bowman's office, God said that very same thing to me.

Dr. Bowman tells me to write down everything I have just experienced. She walks me to the door and in a very, un-Dr. Bowman like fashion, wraps her arms around me. I notice for the first time that she has been weeping as well. She steps back at arm's length and looks up at me. "Mike," she says, "I love you." I am grinning from ear to ear. "Dr. Bowman," I reply, "I know you do."

Chapter 15

GROUP

I have never run to Group before but I am running now. We meet just down the hall, in Dr. Dunning's spacious office. Dr. Rivers is the leader today and I can't wait to tell him, to tell all of them, what has just happened to me.

There are eleven of us in Group today, all men. Last week we had a woman at The Clinic but this week, only men. We come from all parts of the country and a variety of careers. There is a lawyer, a computer engineer, a heavy equipment operator, a teacher and a retired minister. In a strange way, we are family, though except for our common disease we would have never met, and if we had, probably never socialized. Now, we are brothers-in-arms, foxhole buddies, and I am eager to tell them my news.

Our addictions are as varied as our backgrounds. Pornography, prostitution, and pedophilia may be different cancers but they all usually begin with the same defective cell. Some of these men are so addicted to internet porn that they have lost their jobs. A few were frequent customers of prostitutes with all of the dangers and diseases that lifestyle on that level invites. One was a convicted pedophile, here because the court ordered it. From strip clubs to affairs in the church, we were all addicts. We just "acted out" in different ways.

We begin Group, as usual, with a moment of silence, followed by the Serenity Prayer.

"God, grant me the serenity to
accept the things I cannot change,
The courage to change the things I can,
And the wisdom to know the difference."

We take a moment to go around the room and introduce ourselves, and if we desire, tell the nature if our offenses. Although we've done this three times a day for more days than I can count, we go around again and briefly tell how we got here.

"Hi, my name is Frank."

"Hi, Frank."

"I am here because I am a sex addict and I have lost my job and my family."

I wait impatiently for my turn. Finally it comes.

"Hi, my name is Mike."

"Hi Mike."

"I am a sex addict but I have been healed."

Nothing. I expect some shouts of praise, maybe a round of applause, at least some smiles and congratulatory looks. I get nothing. We just move on to the next guy who certainly hasn't made the miraculous breakthrough that I have.

Dr. Rivers opens the discussion today with a reading from the now familiar, still nameless, white book. "The physical and psychological aspects of the addictive process are becoming increasingly identifiable, and sexaholism shares elements in common with other addictions. Our sexual experience or fantasy usually began as 'the answer' to all our needs. It worked. It provided relief and pleasure like nothing else. At some point, most of us came to qualify on all counts as true addicts, and some of us were probably addicted at the very beginning. ..."

"In recovery, we came to see aspects of our sexaholism lying behind the physical and psychological that paralleled similar aspects discovered by recovering alcoholics. These have to do with the personality, dealing with the will and the attitudinal forces shaping the person and character. We refer to this as the *spiritual* dimension" (White Book, 45-46).

He puts down the book and it seems he looks right at me. "I'd like to discuss today the topic, 'Sin or Sickness: Healed or Helped.' By that I mean is your addiction a sin or a sickness? Since there is a spiritual dimension to addiction and recovery, does God heal you or help you?"

The construction worker is the first to speak up, he usually is. He started using pornography as a teen and has spent a fortune in strip clubs. "I believe sexaholism is a disease. Anybody would have to be sick to do some of the stupid things we have all done." We all laugh the uneasy laugh of people who know exactly what he is talking about.

Frank says, "It is a sin. The Bible says clearly we have sinned against God and our own bodies." Frank is here because the court ordered it. A self proclaimed, daily user of pornography, his lust drove him to the most heinous act. He is a retired minister.

Aaron is an attorney from somewhere out west. I know from our talks that he is Jewish but not practicing. He is a heavy user of internet porn and has taken to frequenting prostitutes. He is one of the men in the group that says little but when he does, it is usually right on. "I believe," he says, "That sexaholism is both sin and sickness. We have all learned, during our time here that, like Step One says, 'We were powerless and our lives were out of control.' There is some disease inside each one of us that made us susceptible to the cunning, baffling force of lust. But, like the cancer victim who has cancer after years of smoking, there is also a personal responsibility. Each one of us made choices that were against the will of God. We sinned. I am sick, but I am also a sinner, so I need help and I need to be healed."

That hangs in the air for a minute. Dr. Rivers rarely speaks in Group after opening the meeting and announcing the topic. This is our time and we talk to one another. But today he asks, "How many of you at some point prayed for God to forgive you and to keep you from acting out?" Nearly all of us raised our hands.

"And how many of you tried 'white knuckling' it? Gritting your teeth and by sheer determination vowing to be free from this?" Most of us said yes.

"It seems to me," he presses on, "That Aaron has a good point. If this were just sin you would pray for forgiveness and be okay. If it were just sickness some kind of treatment or program would suffice. Our experience tells us that it takes both. The Second Step of the Twelve Steps says, 'We came to believe that a Power greater than ourselves could deliver us if we asked Him to.' We have learned that sexaholism or lust addiction requires both surrender to God and an ongoing commitment to a program of accountability and support. It is both a sickness and a sin."

I began attending Twelve Step meetings in Miami before I came to The Clinic. The counselors from Harrison suggested that I make ninety meetings in ninety days. The first meeting I found was in the basement of a dilapidated, old, Episcopal Church on the seedy side of town. I went, not because I thought I needed it, or even because I thought it would help. I went because they told me to, and I didn't know what else to do.

I drove around the block several times before I mustered up the courage to go in. I found an open door and walked through the darkened halls until I came to a room where the lights were on. The chairs were in a circle and four grandmotherly-looking ladies were having a quiet conversation. I didn't know what else to do so I asked if this was a meeting for sex addicts. The Episcopal Women's Missionary Group is probably still buzzing about that.

Kindly, they directed me to the right room and I found a seat among twenty men and women of all ages. I sat nervously, not sure what to expect, until one of the men said, "Let's begin with a moment of silence followed by the Serenity Prayer." The meetings were based on the Twelve Steps and Twelve Traditions of Alcoholics Anonymous. I was surprised to find there was a whole network of people around the world that struggled with issues similar to mine. At nearly every meeting, for the first few days, someone read the Twelve Steps:

1. We admitted that we were powerless over our addiction and our lives had become unmanageable.
2. We came to believe that a Power greater than ourselves could restore us to sanity.
3. We made a decision to turn our will and our life over to God.
4. We made a searching and fearless moral inventory of ourselves.
5. We admitted to God, to ourselves, and to another human being, the exact nature of our wrongs.
6. We were entirely ready to have God remove all these defects of character.
7. We humbly asked God to remove our shortcomings.
8. We made a list of all persons we had harmed and became willing to make amends to them all.
9. We made direct amends to such people wherever possible, except where to do so would injure them or others.
10. We continued to take personal inventory, and when we were wrong, promptly admitted it.
11. We sought, through prayer and meditation, to improve our conscious contact with God, praying only for knowledge of His will for us and the power to carry it out.
12. Having had a spiritual awakening, as the result of these steps, we tried to carry the message to others and to practice these principles in all our affairs."

By the third or fourth meeting I had a sponsor and was working on the steps. Doris was gone. The apartment was lonely and full of despair. I had no job, no purpose, nothing to do but wait to come to The Clinic in Scottsdale. I thought I was losing my mind. The meetings were daily islands of sanity in my otherwise insane world. Most of each day was spent reading the Big Book and writing out each Step.

The only apparent rules of the meeting were absolute honesty and complete acceptance. It was a place to go where I could tell the truth and feel no condemnation or judgment. Every one there had a story to tell that was as shameful and as crazy as mine. After one meeting, when I had confessed that I never in my life felt like I fit in with any group, one man came up to me and said, "Congratulations, this is a group of insane, selfish, lying, cheating, lust addicts. You've finally found a place where you belong." We both laughed and I knew then that no matter the outcome of anything else, I want to commit to a Twelve Step way of life.

Dr. Rivers interrupts my daydreaming by asking again, "So if our addiction is both sickness and sin, then are we healed or helped? Are we healed in layers? Does God do a little healing at a time?" I know he is talking to me.

I think back to the vision of less than an hour ago. I am healed. I know that. God loves me. He has delivered me. I am completely healed. My heart wells with joy at the thought of it. But if I am healed, then why attend meetings, and work the steps, and have a sponsor? On the other hand, I know, from what I have gone through, that even with "help," I cannot work my way out of my addiction. I need both help and healing. I speak up, "We are both. There is no recovery without the miraculous healing of our Higher Power. In fact, in my last session, God healed me. I came in here excited to tell you all that." The faces in the room are bright-eyed with tears of hope. They had heard me. "But," I continue, "I am also helped. This disease is so insidious that I know it will come back the second I let down my guard. I must be diligent to attend meetings, work the steps, and stay accountable for the rest of my life. I am no different from the heart patient who is healed by open heart surgery but commits to a lifestyle of exercise and healthy diet. I have been healed and by God's help, I have the hope that I will stay that way."

I can tell by the look on Dr. Rivers' face that I got it right. Healing is essential but it does not end there. To just claim to be helped is to miss all that God has done. He smiles and nods, then asks me a strange question but immediately I know what he is getting at.

"Who are you, Mike?" he asks.

I am searching for the word. There has to be something, not healed, not helped.

When I was growing up in South Carolina, I used to laugh at some of the "mispronunciations" and miss-sayings of the Pee Dee area people. They called a paper sack a "poke." They referred to taking someone in a car as "carrying" them, like "Can you carry me to the store?" And they always pronounced the word "help" like it was "hope." I would here people say to my dad, "Preacher, can you hope me?"

It all comes together for me. I am what I am by the grace of God, on both sides of The Clinic. God brought me through all of this, to this point, and if I let Him, He will see me through to the end. To leave here, free from addiction, as marvelous as that is, is not all that He has in mind. I have a future. I am reminded of Jeremiah 29:11.It says, "I know the plans I have for you, says the Lord, plans to bless you and not to harm you, plans to give you a future and hope." That's the word I am looking for.

I reply to Dr. River's question, "I am an addict but I have been hoped!"

Chapter 16

LADIES BIBLE STUDY

Group runs over the allotted time today and Dr. Heinz is looking for me when I return to the waiting room. It is a strange sensation to see this very professional looking, attractive counselor sitting on a cracked, fake, leather chair in the room full of "inmates," thumbing through a magazine. From the look on her face, I guess she is more than a little relieved to see that I made it through the night. It dawns on me that she really is concerned and, I must have been closer to the brink of destruction than I realize. She greets me with a smile and a firm handshake. I follow her across the street to her office.

The late morning heat is a welcome change from the air conditioned building. The Clinic is always on the verge of too cool. The sky is cloudless, brilliant blue, and I can't remember when the flowering trees, that line the street, looked better. I am thinking, "It is a wonderful day to be alive." My wife has left me. My children disowned me. I have no home, no job, no income, and I am thinking, "It is a wonderful day to be alive."

We enter her office and immediately Dr. Heinz asks me if I wrote the letter to God. I have nearly forgotten it, in the mystery of the morning, but I take it out now and hand it to her. To my surprise, she does not unfold it, or even look down at it. She reaches in her desk and pulls out a plain white envelope. She places the letter inside and licks the flap to seal the envelope shut. Then Dr. Heinz hands the envelope back to me.

"Only you and God know the contents of that letter," she says. "And unless you feel like you should share it with someone else, it will always be that way. Now, how do you feel?"

It is the question I have been waiting for. Yesterday afternoon, in this same office, I unleashed a tidal wave of agony, despair, and hopelessness. Today I am gushing, overflowing with joy, amazement, and an awareness of God's love for me that I have never known. I bubble and ramble and spew and spout. I tell her nonstop of the awful night, of the phone call from Dortha Mae, about the EMDR, and my vision of God. I tell her about Frank, and the verse from Zephaniah. I explain the discussion in Group, and my realization of being both healed and helped. I am weeping and laughing, gesturing wildly and sitting on the edge of my seat. The incredible, nearly indescribable, powerful, passionate miracle of the morning comes pouring out in a tearful torrent of wonder. At last, out of words and out of breath, I stop.

Her eyes are welling with tears and her smile nearly matches mine, as Dr. Heinz says, "That is wonderful, Mike. I was so worried yesterday. I prayed for you all during the night."

I am beginning to see with new eyes--she cares about me. Not just her. Dr. Rivers cares about me. Dr. Dunning, and Andie Bowman, and even the psychiatrist, they care about me. God has surrounded me with people who are genuinely concerned for my healing. It has been this way my whole life. Only now, He has opened my eyes and I can see that.

But Dr. Heinz is still a counselor, and counselors ask the hard questions. "What now, Mike? What about Doris? What about your family?"

Like a man awaking from a wonderful dream before he has to go to work, it dawns on me that I don't have the answer to that question. In fact, until this very moment, I have not considered that question. For the last two hours I have been reveling in my own personal deliverance and rejoicing in the healing that I am sure God has given me. I must admit that I have not been thinking much about anyone else. Now I do.

"I believe they will be happy for me," I respond. "I think they will see me and know that I am a changed man."

"I believe you are right," says Dr. Heinz, "but they have still been deeply hurt. They may be happy for you, but may not be willing to let you back into their lives."

It is amazing that you would pay someone two-hundred dollars an hour to take all of the wind out of your sails and make you go from feeling euphoric to feeling like the scum of the earth. I just assumed that, since I was healed, everything would be right with the world, at least with my world.

"That's the point," says Dr. Heinz. "It is not your world. It is God's world. And you will have to surrender yourself to His will whatever that means. The Third Step says, 'We made a decision to turn our will and our life over to the care of God.' Mike, here is the test. You have discovered now that God loves you. Are you willing to trust His love and accept whatever He has in store for you?"

The giddy, happy, enthusiastic joy is gone. But I have still been healed. I still have hope. I am just as sure of my vision as I was two hours ago. I do not hesitate. "Yes," I answer in a voice that is soft, but I hope, confident. "Yes, I have proven that I will screw my life up every time I try to run it. Now it is God's. If my family responds positively, or if they don't, I will spend the rest of my life trying to know, and follow, His plan for me."

Dr. Heinz nods. She opens my file and searches for something then picks up the black phone on her desk. "Let's call Doris and invite her to fly out here for a few days."

I can't breathe. My eyes will not focus because of the tears. I am terrified and elated. I simply nod.

A few days after I left Miami to fly to The Clinic, Doris drove back down to our apartment on the third hole of the world class golf course. When she and Jacob left, they were in such a hurry that they left most of their clothes and personal items behind. This seemed like a good time to return to the apartment and remove her belongings. We had talked about it on the phone and, I agreed that it made sense.

God had been doing a great work in Doris during the weeks that we were in Miami together. She had been voraciously reading books by Beth Moore. Her own, personal, quiet time had taken on a new dimension as God braced her for the pain that I was putting her through. But it was the Ladies Bible Study that had the most powerful influence on my wife. She would attend each Thursday morning and stay for hours. She would come home blessed and, often at supper, tell me everything that was said, every chorus that they sang, every scripture they quoted. Those ladies became a refuge to Doris.

Her return to Miami was only partially to gather her belongings. She also wanted to attend the Ladies Bible Study one more time. She arranged her trip so that she would be there on Thursday morning and, surprise them by driving up to the house just as they were beginning to sing. The door was open and through the screen they saw her get out of the car. Doris said later, it was like bees pouring out of a hive, those black, island ladies came pouring out of the door and surrounded her with shouts, and hugs, and kisses. It was such a God thing that, in a time when she felt so alone and rejected, God would give her this moment of overwhelming love and affection.

They nearly carried her back inside and, for the next ninety minutes, there were no problems, no struggles, no unfaithful husbands or broken promises. For the next ninety minutes there was only unending praise and worship of the One that she was learning to really trust. Dortha Mae quoted scripture. Sister Rachel prayed. They all sang, old hymns and new worship choruses, *a capella*, a little off key, but they sang, and God filled the room.

They would stop to ask about the boys, about her job, and even about Pastor Mike. She would tell them the news and then, without judgment or comment, they would pray, and sing, and worship again.

Finally, the Bible Study came to an end. The island ladies embraced Doris and pledged to keeping giving her their love and continued prayers. As she stood to leave, Miss Grace approached her. The Ladies Bible Study met in Miss Grace's home and that made her the *de facto* leader of the group. She was in her late sixties, a godly woman, from Jamaica. She, like most of the others had come to America, raised a family and made a life for them, pretty much on her own. They were strong women, with tender hearts, and Miss Grace was the strongest and most tender of all. She came over to Doris and put her hands on Doris's face, black hands against white cheeks. She turned Doris's face until they were inches apart and they were looking directly into one another's eyes. Then, in a voice that was barely above a whisper, with her Jamaican accent evident in every word, Miss Grace sang into Doris's heart.

"What a friend we have in Jesus,
All our sins and griefs to bear.
What a privilege to carry
Everything to God in prayer.
Oh, what peace we often forfeit.
Oh, what needless pain we bear.
All because we do not carry
Everything to God in prayer."

The room was so quiet that you could hear the ladies breathing. Birds whistled in the Florida palms outside. Doris said it felt as if angel wings were softly stirring the air. Miss Grace sang the verse.

"Have we trial and temptations?
Is there trouble anywhere?
We must never be discouraged.
Take it to the Lord in prayer.
Can we friend a friend so faithful
Who will all our sorrows share?
Jesus knows our every weakness.
Take it to the Lord in prayer."

The other ladies gathered around and just as softly began to sing.

> "Are we weak and heavy laden,
> Cumbered with a load of care?
> Precious Savior, still our refuge,
> Take it to the Lord in prayer.
> Do thy friends despise, forsake thee,
> Take it to the Lord in prayer.
> In His arms He'll take and shield thee,
> Thou wilt find a solace there."
>
> (*What A Friend We Have In Jesus,*
> Joseph Scriven, public domain)

An old, old hymn became as meaningful on that day as when it was written a hundred years earlier. Doris imagined these precious black ladies had whispered this song through many trials of their own. It was their prayer, their gift to Doris. And it was God's gift to her as well.

Dr. Heinz reached Doris at work. She briefly introduced herself and explained that I was in the room at that moment. She offered very little explanation and certainly did not brag on me the way I thought she should. She simply said, "Doris, we believe it is time for you to come to The Clinic. Can you come next week?"

I didn't notice that I was squeezing a pillow so tight that my fingers hurt. They say that time often stands still during moments of great stress and I can tell you it is true. The seconds seemed like hours. I could hear the traffic noise outside the office window and the buzzing of the fluorescent light in the ceiling. I could hear my own heart beat. I could also hear Doris's voice, though muffled, as Dr. Heinz held the receiver away from her ear. Softly she said, "Yes, I can come. I will be there on Monday."

Chapter 17

PLAY ACTING

The weekend is lost in nervous anticipation and activity. Counseling and Group continues on Saturday but, try as I might to
focus, I am consumed by my fears and hopes for Monday. I am
trying to learn to live in the moment, to face one challenge, one
day, one minute at a time, but this weekend, I cannot help but
look ahead to what Monday might bring, and how Doris will
respond.

The staff at The Clinic sent a car to the airport for her and now
we sit on opposite ends of the couch, in the big office, waiting
for Carl Rivers to come in. I am glad that our first encounter is at
Group. It makes it less threatening. I don't think she'll kill me in
front of so many witnesses. I have introduced her proudly to the
other "inmates." I felt a strange sense of urgency for her to meet
the rest of the men at The Clinic, as if, by seeing them, I might
appear less vile to her. They, in turn, have taken on a new air. Each
man acts more respectful and almost timid in her presence. I think
I understand. They see their own spouses in her face.

I glance nervously over at Doris. She looks down at her hands.
We have tried to make small talk but that seemed like a wasted
effort. There is too much at stake to spend emotional energy
discussing the air traffic over Phoenix or the weather in Nashville.
I imagine she is wondering how we got to this point, and who this

strange creature is beside her. I am wondering how we got to this point, and who this strange creature is beside her.

We both relax a little with relief when Dr. Rivers comes in. He introduces himself to Doris, and settles in to his favorite chair and then begins Group as usual, with a moment of silence followed by the Serenity Prayer. We go around the room, each man telling his name and the nature of his offense. I steal glances at Doris from time to time as she listens to the brief stories that I have heard so many times already.

Introductions over, Dr. Rivers turns his attention to Doris. I see a side of him, an attentiveness, that I have not seen. The yellow legal pad remains on his desk. He leans forward when she speaks and listens to her responses. Like the Evaluation, I am relegated to the role of spectator, welcome to stay and observe but not allowed to speak.

After a few pleasantries, he asks his favorite question: "Doris, what do you make up about all of this?"

Doris has a way of expressing the painful truth without coming across as angry or vindictive. She begins by saying, "Michael is a wonderful father. He loves the boys and has raised them to be good, godly young men. He is an excellent pastor and teacher. Everyone loves him and every place we have been the church has grown tremendously."

Dr. Rivers interrupts her, "What about you, though? How has he been to you, Doris?"

Again her tender disposition takes over. "He has always been a perfect gentleman to me. He opens the door for me and is thoughtful about even the smallest things."

Carl stops her again. "Doris," he says, "You sound like you are talking about the husband of the year. This man has wrecked your life. He has cheated on you at least three times. He has cost you your home at least twice. He has wasted years and years of the time you should have spent together. How does that make you feel?"

She does not look at me. I think this would be easier for her if I were not in the room. I know it would be easier for me. The other men in Group shift in their chairs. I think they are hearing something they do not want to hear. She begins to weep and forced honesty overrides her natural tendency to protect. She begins to tell the truth.

Doris grew up in a very conservative, Christian home in the hills of Tennessee. Her parents were two of the most saintly people I had ever known. Her father especially loves God and easily accepts Him as Lord of the universe. Every decision that is made, is made "Lord willing," and every good thing that happens deserves a "Thank God." He sees the world as black and white, either you mind God or you did not, and offers no quarter to those who are unwilling, or unable, to live life "by The Book."

Her mother had passed away a few years before we moved to Harrison and Doris had grown even closer to her father. We went back often to the old home place, where the extended family gathered for Memorial Day cookouts and Fourth of July croquet. They are a tight knit family, bonded closely together by their deep faith and their unquestioning respect and love for their father. I feel proud to be a part of them and always a little envious at what I had missed as a child.

A few weeks before we moved to Miami, we had gone to the farm to visit her father. He was aware of our struggle and could feel the tension in Doris and me as we talked. In his straight forward approach, he asked if we were both "close to God" and if our marriage was solid. Doris confessed to him her suspicions and concerns but admitted she had no proof for anything she felt. She wept as she asked him to pray for us, for me, and I sat, an uncomfortable spectator, during her whole conversation.

Her father then turned to me, without judging, just expecting an answer, asked me directly, "Is any of this true?"

I looked him right in the eyes and, without hesitation, lied like a pirate. "No," I said. And in my most sympathetic voice went on to explain how I understood why Doris would feel this way. I told him about the minor "mistakes" I had made in judgment and how my busyness in the church had kept me from being as attentive to his daughter as I should have been. I apologized profusely and asked him to pray that I would "do better."

Because things were black and white with him, he seemed to accept my explanation, prayed for our home and ministry, and sent us on our way with his blessing.

As Doris tells her side of my story, it becomes apparent that this event seems to hold great pain for her. Every failure, every indiscretion, every blatant act is small in comparison to the flagrant lies I told her father. She seems genuinely incredulous that I could have done such a thing.

She has been talking for less than thirty minutes but it feels longer to me. I look in the faces of the other men in the room, expecting condemnation. Instead they all look ashamed. When she finishes, one by one they all express the same thought.

"For the first time I understand how I hurt my wife."

"You made me see that my lies and sins were so damaging to the entire family. I don't know if they will ever forgive me."

"I am so sorry for the pain that you felt. I feel like I am responsible too."

Carl seizes the moment. "How do you feel about some play acting?" he asks the group. Without waiting for a response, he opens a closet and takes out a fat, red, plastic whiffle bat. I am not so sure about the play acting now.

He brings Doris to the center of the room and gives her the bat. He has her stand in front of one of the couches and piles it high with the overstuffed pillows. The men all gather around her and, at his instruction, begin to shout at her, words that she used in her story about me.

"I lied to you."

"I cost you your security."

"I cheated on you."

"I made you feel ugly."

All of the men, except me. I am again a spectator as she endures this verbal barrage of the things I had done to her literally. When it seems that none of us can take it any more, Carl instructs Doris to begin to beat the pillow with the bat. She shouts, (if Doris can shout) statements of personal affirmation and vindication.

"I don't have to take this from you."

"I am worth more than this."

"I deserve to be treated better than this."

Each statement is accompanied by a blow to the pillows. They become more severe and heartfelt as the play acting continues. It only lasts for a few minutes but it is an emotionally agonizing exercise. By the time they finish, Doris and the men in her cast are weeping. And I am sitting in the corner, too devastated to talk. I have been reading the "Twelve Steps" several times a day and only now the eighth step becomes meaningful. It says, "We made a list of all persons we had harmed and became willing to make amends to them all." For all of the healing and hope that I felt last week, I realize now more than ever, that there is a world of recovery left for me, and a lifetime of making amends.

Carl dismisses the group and asks Doris and me to stay. The men file out quietly, a few pat Doris on the back or tentatively touch her arm. No one looks at me. When they are gone, Dr. Rivers says, "Doris, Mike has come a long way in his time here. I believe he is on the road to recovery. The question is, are you willing to walk that road with him? That is what you will have to decide and no one will blame you, whatever your choice. You have obviously been wounded. For years the method of operation for you both has been to sweep things under the carpet and go on. In fact, even your faith says you should forgive and forget. The problem with that is, that wounds ignored become festering boils under the skin that will erupt at some point in the future. Until we admit that we are sick, we will never be able to get well. Mike has been sick, and he has made you sick. Your healing will not come until you are willing to acknowledge that."

We sit, lost in thought for a moment. I do not know what Doris is thinking but I pray silently that she will be healed and that I will still be around to see it. My only hope is that the God, who has become so real to her, will intervene once again. I guess that I will have to, as she has, put my trust in Him.

Dr. Rivers gives us a minute to collect our thoughts and then asks, "Doris, are you ready to move on?" Without giving her a chance to respond, he opens the door and sends us to the waiting room.

Chapter 18

THE CONTRACT

After a few days, Doris has settled into the same routine that I have been in for awhile now. We get up before it is light, have a breakfast of cold cereal or instant oatmeal, get ready, and walk the blocks to The Clinic. The motel room is crowded. We debated on whether or not two rooms would be more appropriate but a tight budget and twenty-five years of marriage prevailed. Each night we lay carefully on our own side of the just barely double bed and try to sleep without turning over.

Actually, we are beginning to talk and even laugh a little, and I am hopeful. The walk to The Clinic takes a little longer with Doris along, but it is one of the highlights of my day. For fifty minutes or so, we act like we used to when we were college kids, chatting about our parents, about church life, now, about the boys, but not about the future. She doesn't bring it up, and I am trying not to push. At times, as we walk, our arms brush and we find ourselves walking hand in hand. Often she asks about the treatment at The Clinic. I tell her with great detail about each session. I have always been able to make her laugh and I do impressions of Dr. Dunning and Carl Rivers.

This morning we have stopped on the bench across from The Clinic and I am telling her about "the vision." I have told her bits and pieces already, but this is the first time I describe everything.

I describe the picture of Joshua on the beach. I tell her about the scene where Josh and Jacob are grown men. Just talking about it brings back the elation of that moment, when God Himself said to me, "I love you and I have always loved you." Tears of joy drip from the end of my nose as I talk and Doris is just as moved. I am sure that no matter the outcome of our marriage, her most sincere prayer has been for my healing.

She questions me over and over about the various scenes in my vision, what they meant, how they affected me. I read her the letter I wrote to God and the Bible verse in Zephaniah that Frank shared with me. She is beaming as I tell her about the call from Dortha Mae and the prayer that Dortha prayed over me. It is a moment that I do not want to end, but the doors are opening at The Clinic and, our first session today is with Kay Heinz. We are scheduled to write our separation contract.

Doris and Jacob went back to a part of the country we always called home after our separation, middle Tennessee. Her family lives there and it was a safe place to be. Jacob moved in with his brother, into a small house that Joshua had bought in the area. Doris moved in with her sister. She found a job working for some wonderful, godly friends, who loved her and helped her get back on her feet. She began to think about putting the pieces of her life back together. Her devotional life continued to flourish.

On Sunday mornings, she and Jacob would meet and go to church together. They found a large, dynamic church on the edge of town, with a killer music program. Doris said that every Sunday the spirit of worship comforted her, soothed her broken heart. She and Jacob began to look forward to those Sunday services as much as any other event in their lives.

Just a week ago, on Sunday, they arrived a little late for church and were forced to find a seat in the balcony. The music began, and as usual, God began to bless them both with His presence. Suddenly, a man stood directly behind them and began to speak out loud in a strange, but attractive language. Doris had never heard anyone speak in tongues before but knew immediately that this was taking place now. The music stopped. The choir was silent. Three thousand faces turned to look right over Doris and Jacob, to the man behind them.

He spoke a few sentences and then there was silence. It was only a matter of seconds until another voice spoke from the other side of the vast auditorium. The interpretation, on that morning spoke straight into Doris's heart. "My child," the interpreter said, "The chains of bondage that have been on you and your family for generations, is now broken. I have delivered you and removed your yoke. You, and all those who come after you, are now free."

Doris and Jacob looked at each other with wonder and joy. They knew that the message was for them. At that moment they both felt sure that I would be healed and God would restore our family. They went home and called Joshua and told him all that they had seen and heard. It was the only time, in the months that they attended that church, that anything like that ever happened. That was last Sunday, just before the voodoo machine vision on Thursday. Doris had no way of knowing, nor did I, that this epiphany, this gift from God, would be the first day of the most miraculous week in our lives.

Each day this week has brought changes in both of us. I am learning to live honestly, even about my emotions. When I am on top of the struggles, I express that. When I am just about buried under the guilt, and shame, and regret, I express that as well. I have felt before that I had to keep my "game face" on all of the time or my family would lose respect for me. They would not love me if they knew I was human. Now I am learning that, in order to stay healthy and healed, I must be open, honest, and transparent about who I am.

Doris, on the other hand, seems to be learning that she does not have to comfort me. She is allowing me to be down without feeling like she has to pick me up. At first, I resented that, but I am realizing that it takes a great deal of pressure off of our relationship. My health and happiness is not dependant on her response to me. Nor is it her responsibility.

Each day Doris has gone through a plethora of emotions. Her anger is finally starting to come out. They tell me that is a good thing, though some days I'm not sure. She is able to express her frustration without worrying that it will set me back. She has even been able to admit that she sees a change in me. Moment by moment, we both seem to be growing more hopeful about the future.

The greatest change I see in Doris is that she has discovered her voice. She says what she is thinking. She offers her opinion. She stands up and disagrees with me, with the other "inmates," even with the counselors. One day we were in Group and the therapist of the day, Dr. Dunning, made a comment about fixing our marriage. Doris spoke up and said, "Let me tell you, we are not here to fix marriages. I tried for years to fix my marriage and found it was impossible to do. What we need to do instead is fix our eyes on Jesus." She started quoting Beth Moore and the Apostle Paul and Gloria Gaither. By the time she was done, she was standing in the middle of the room and the rest of us were ready to take up an offering and go to the altar. We all clapped when she sat down, and I thought I had never been more proud of her. At that moment, I was pretty sure we were going to make it.

We have seen Kay Heinz a couple of times since Doris has been here. Today she is working with us on a separation contract. I would rather work on a back-together contract or an act-like-it-never-happened contract, but all of the counselors seem to feel this is the right approach to take.

We agree to remain separated for three more months. During that time, we will talk on the phone daily. I will continue counseling sessions every other week and Twelve Step meetings twice a week. I will move back to middle Tennessee in a month and try to find a house for us to live in. I will see Doris and the boys on weekends and we will work together on some family assignments that The Clinic will send home with me.

It seems so formal and contrived, but I am not in a position to argue the point. I am so eager to get my family back that I am willing to do whatever is necessary. There is also a new sense of meekness that has come with my healing. I am sure that I don't have all of the answers but, at last, I don't feel like I have to act like I do.

We end the session by compiling a list of "red light" actions. Commit any one of these, for the rest of my life, and the whole deal is off. There is no second chance, no grace period. For as long as I live, a single action on my part from this list, and my wife and my children will walk away and never look back. I open my mouth to protest but one look from my wife and my counselor reminds me that these are non-negotiable issues.

- I will never have any contact of any kind with the "other woman." If I am contacted by her I will say, "I do not want to talk to you," and hang up.
- I will have no sexual or intimate contact with any person other than my wife for the rest of my life.
- I will be on the alert for "flirting" either from me or towards me and talk to my wife about it immediately.
- I will tell the truth about everything, all the time, to everybody, in every circumstance.

I write the red light rules in my journal and mark the top of the page, DO NOT EVER FORGET. Both Doris and I sign the bottom of this page and the bottom of the separation contract. There is a solemnity about this moment. I feel like we should light a candle or something. Kay says, "As you continue in your recovery, Mike, you may come to feel that these rules are juvenile and demeaning. You may feel like you have grown beyond them and it is insulting to still have to 'check' yourself. Remember, you have surrendered your will to God. For the rest of your life, it is not about you. God has answered a miraculous prayer for you. Now you have to keep your promises to Him."

With that introduction, she opens a faded, paperback Bible that is on her desk. Doris and I stand with our hands together over the contract that we have just written. Kay says, "I want you to recite these words with me. They are from the sixty-fifth Psalm."

She gives us the psalm one line at a time and we repeat it back to her. "We will fulfill our vows to you, O God, for you answer our prayers. Though our hearts are filled with sins, you forgive them all. You faithfully answer our prayers with awesome deeds." She flips over a few pages and reads from Psalm one-hundred-seven. "Then they cried to the Lord in their trouble and He saved them from their distress. He sent out His Word and healed them, and delivered them from destruction. Let them thank the Lord for His steadfast love and His wonderful works to humankind."

Tears are flowing again. My heart is pounding in my chest and my head is buzzing with exhilaration. I believe every word Kay has read. I believe that what God says, He will do. Just to be standing here with my wife beside me is amazing. It is proof that He has done some awesome things. But I have a feeling that His awesome deeds have only begun.

Chapter 19

GRADUATION

The waiting room is empty this afternoon except for Doris and me, the receptionist behind the formica counter, and the dusty, fake, ferns. I am trying to remember how many days I have been at The Clinic, and how many Evaluations I have endured. I am not sure. I do know that this last week, with Doris here, has been a smorgasbord of feelings. Some days, some hours, have been nearly euphoric highs as we laughed at our personality quirks and made tentative plans for the future. Other sessions took us back into the valley of despair, wallowing in old hurts and rehearsing painful, painful failures.

I am amazed at Doris. She has exhibited an inner strength, a quiet confidence that I have never seen in her before. There is an understanding and an intuitive wisdom in her that has impressed the counselors and endeared her to the other men in my group. Her honest assessment of where we have been, and where we are now, opened the eyes of the rest of the "inmates" so that, Doris has been as much a part of their healing as anything else that has taken place this week.

Each man today has gone through Evaluation. We are the last. Charles stopped by a few minutes ago, on his way out. He is headed back to Texas and his construction business. His wife agreed to give him another chance. He hugs Doris and shakes my hand, too emotional to speak. Before him, Frank came out and sat beside us, too close, and talked for awhile, too loud. His wife has filed for divorce. His children have sent word they want nothing to do with him. He is going to an empty apartment in Colorado where he will wear a bracelet on his ankle to track his movements for the next six months. He holds our hands and we pray together, then he slips out the door.

One by one, each man passes us. A few will stay on at The Clinic for another week. Most are going home with the hope that life will be better, that they will be better. They are good men. I have learned much from them, and from their stories. We have exchanged phone numbers and e-mail addresses, though we all know that we will probably never contact each other again. This chapter in our lives is finished.

The last man out, before we go in, is Aaron, the Jewish attorney. It has been a difficult time for him and I am especially worried about his continued sobriety. He is single now. His wife left several months ago. His law practice will keep him busy but I wonder about the lonely nights ahead and how he will cope. Doris has talked to him often this week. She gave him one of her Beth Moore books. I know she has shared her faith with him a few times. One day he asked her in Group, "How will you ever trust your husband again?" She said to him, to all of us, softly and instantly, "I do not have to trust my husband. I have transferred my trust to God."

Aaron comes out of Evaluation and sees us across the waiting room. He heads straight for us and, as we stand, embraces us both in a big, bone cracking, bear hug. He is holding the book that Doris gave him and he opens it for us to see that he has written our names and the date on the inside cover. He steps back and heads for the door, then seems to remember something. He looks at Doris and says, "It's Friday. I have not been to Temple in twenty-five years. Because of you, I'm going tonight."

The waiting room door opens and Dr. Rivers pokes his head out. "Mike and Doris, we are ready for you now."

Evaluation, even on the last day, is still an intimidating ordeal. There are more counselors than usual today. Dr. Dunning is in his customary place, behind his desk in the corner. Kay Heinz and Andie Bowman are sitting together on a sofa, under the picture of Dr. Dunning fly fishing in Canada. Dr. Bell, the psychiatrist, looks more like Al Pacino than ever in a pullover sweater and a tweed jacket. Carl Rivers has taken a seat at the end of the room beside two empty chairs and he motions for us to sit next to him.

The counselors and therapists may be smiling a little more than they usually are today, but it is lost on me. I still feel like a kid in the principal's office. I am too nervous to look anyone in the eye. Doris reaches over and squeezes my hand and I relax a bit. Maybe they won't tell me I've flunked the fifth grade and am being held back.

This is my last day at the clinic. I don't know what I am feeling. For the first time in my whole life, I know that God loves me. The verse that says "we are new creatures in Christ" has come alive for me. But I have so much ground yet to cover. I am like a computer that has had a whole new operating system installed but is still full of the same old files. Everything in my head seems to be working smoother and better but, every once in a while, I hit a button and all of the old garbage pops up on the screen. I have been reprogrammed. Now, and from now on, I will be at work replacing the broken files with the new, correct ones. Am I ready for that? Maybe I should stay here a little longer? What if I go outside and fail?

I think of a scene in a movie, <u>The Truman Show</u>. Jim Carey is the central figure, Truman, who has lived his whole life in a false, artificial, world, constructed for him, and viewed by a television audience of millions. He has discovered that everything he thought and believed is wrong, and in the last scene he is sitting in a boat, ready to climb out and walk through a door, into the "real" world. He asks the producer, "Was nothing real?" To which the producer responds, "You were real."

I feel like that is where I am now. The world that I have constructed in my mind is messed up and deeply flawed, but it is my world. I am familiar with it. I know how it operates and what the rules are. I know where to go to get rid of pain and how to cope when things aren't going my way. I am in control in my world.

At The Clinic, I have discovered that my world is not real--it is fake and phony. I have discovered that there is a wonderful, healthy world waiting outside of my head and all I have to do is get out of the boat and walk through the door. And I have discovered that I have it in me to be real, genuine, no secrets, no pretense, real.

In the movie, Cristos, the director, talks to Truman and tries to convince him to stay inside the artificial world. "There is no more truth out there than in the world I constructed for you here. The same lies, the same deceit. Here," he says. "Everything is taken care of for you. All of your wishes and desires are provided for. You have nothing to fear." That is where the comparison breaks down.

In my world, Christ has always wanted to be the director but I have not allowed Him to. And in my story, Christ is the One encouraging me to get out of the boat, walk through the door into the bright, wonderful, new world that He has prepared for me. In this new world, Christ is not just with me in the boat, but out of the boat, out of the phony world. He is with me in everything I do.

Dr. Dunning interrupts my daydreaming. He is speaking to the counselors around the room as if Doris and I were not there. "These guys were pretty hopeless when Mike came here. He had managed to make wrong, destructive, decisions at almost every turn, so often that he nearly destroyed his wife and children." If this is going to be an encouraging speech, he has some work to do.

"Mike came from a background where he was so beat down, and so abandoned that he had no hope. He could not believe that anyone would ever be able to love him. He is responsible for every sin he has ever committed but, he was set up to fail from early childhood. His belief system has led him to lie, and deceive, and hide his true feelings in order to make people like him. He is a mess."

The other counselors in the room nod in agreement. I have the feeling, though I do not look, that Doris is nodding too. If we are getting ready to vote on whether or not I get to go home, it's not looking good for the home team right now.

Dr. Dunning turns to me and suddenly I am the center of everyone's attention. "Mike," he says, "The church doesn't know what to do with you. We are not equipped to handle men or women who are such huge failures. We preach grace and repentance and good news for their laypeople but for their leaders there is little tolerance for sin, sickness and stupidity. You have demonstrated all three." Now, that should cheer me up.

He goes on: "That doesn't make the church bad. We just don't know what to do." He stands up and comes around the desk, pacing the middle of the room as he talks. "I believe that God has brought you and Doris through this trial for a reason. You could have been smarter and stayed out of this mess, but since you didn't, I think God has a plan for you. You have a message. He has given you a new voice. And the cruelest thing in the world would be for him to give you a new voice without allowing you to speak."

Something in that last phrase grips my heart and the now familiar tears begin to fall again. "You must live the rest of your days practicing rigorous honesty. Anything short of that is to set yourself up to fall again. We have given you tools here to maintain your sobriety and to grow your relationship with Doris and your boys to a place you haven't known before." I realize that Doris is still holding my hand. I glance over to see her tears falling as well.

"You must surround yourself with people who will keep you honest and centered. Your Twelve Step Group will become your extended family. Stay close to them. Depend on them. Use their collective wisdom to make the right choices from here on out. If you do these things, God will use you. He is not finished with you and Doris. In fact, he may have just begun. I have a feeling that this failure may be the most significant tool God wants you to employ in the days ahead. You may be a little beat up but you have a powerful story to tell."

He goes to his desk and takes out a beaten up, brown envelope, about the size of a legal pad. It was crumpled and torn and as he brought it closer I could see it was nearly covered with postage stamps and marks. "I got this in the mail a few weeks ago," he says. "Inside was a book from a friend of mine in Africa. He mailed it months before but it had been lost for quite some time. As you can see, when it finally arrived, it was pretty beat up. I don't know where it had been or what had happened to it. But it arrived, and the book inside was worth the wait."

Now he is immediately in front of me, his arm extended so that I can clearly see the tattered envelope. "There is a message that is stamped on this envelope. I believe it is just for you. I remembered this old package this morning and God told me to show it to you today." He puts on his reading glasses and points at one, purple, stamped statement in the lower right-hand corner. It says, "Damaged in transition but still deliverable."

There is no graduation ceremony, no certificate, no pomp and circumstance, at the end of my time at The Clinic. The counselors make their final Evaluation, the receptionist hands you the bill and you are on your way off the boat , through the door and into a brand-new world. When Dr. Dunning is finished speaking, Carl Rivers stands, opens the door and waits for Doris and me to follow him. He walks us to the waiting room and shakes my hand. It is not a perfunctory, businesslike handshake. He takes my hand and, with his other hand, grabs my wrist. "Mike," he says, "God has been good to you. He is not finished with you. I can't wait to see what next looks like." With that he is back inside The Clinic. No goodbye, or good luck.

One night, while we were in Arizona, Doris and I rented a movie to watch in the motel room. I'm not sure we picked the best one, *Diary of a Mad Black Woman*. It was a movie about a wife who has been cheated on and mistreated by her husband. There are guns involved and house fires. I was thinking at the time that Doris might be getting some good ideas. But in one scene near the end the grandmother in the movie is talking to the young wife. As you would expect the young woman is devastated and depressed and believing her life is over. She can't forget all that she has lost. Grandmother gives here perfect advice. "You need to stop thinking about what you think you lost and start looking forward to what is ahead of you." It has become the theme for Doris and me as we prepare to leave The Clinic and go our separate ways.

This afternoon Doris and I will catch a cab to the airport. She will fly back to middle Tennessee and me to Miami. We have a contract to work on and a lifetime of healing to do. But we have learned to surrender everything to God. It's in His hands now. As we stand on the sidewalk, mustering our energy for the walk back to the motel, a cab pulls up. From the back steps a man in his mid-forties. He has on a Gamecocks sweatshirt. That is the mascot of the University of South Carolina so I guess he has just flown in from my home state. His face is drawn and pale, and etched with the pain of a failed life, and a failing marriage. He looks a little bit confused and turns to me. "I'm looking for The Clinic," he says in an accent I recognize from my youth. "Can you hope me?"

"No," I say, "But they can in there."

Chapter 20

TWO-YEAR CHIP

I am sitting in my regular seat, a rusty, old desk chair with the wheels off. It rocks a little too far back so that if you are not careful, you will tip over in the middle of a meeting. The basement of this church has become a familiar "home away from home" for me these last twenty-four months. At least once a week, but usually two or three times, we gather here in the youth room, sitting in hand-me-down furniture, with posters on the walls. The long, skinny windows look out at ground level so that all you can see when you are seated is the tops of the weeds growing against the outside wall of the church.

There are fourteen of us tonight. Sometimes as many as twenty gather. Sometimes as few as three or four. There is a contractor in our group, a teacher, a truck driver and two ex-ministers. I know everyone here tonight although I still forget the names of a couple of the new guys until we go around the room and introduce ourselves. After two years, I am one of the senior members of the group, not by age, although that's close, but by seniority. A lot of guys have come and gone during this time. Some moved away. Some just quit coming. We don't go after them. We have learned that until a person is desperate for his or her sobriety over everything else, there really isn't much that we can do.

Pornography has captured most of these men. The internet, with its easy access and built in anonymity, is a breeding ground for sexual addiction. I have been amazed, in my two years here, at the number of new "clients" that come through our meeting, and at how young many of them are. Often, they come and go, unwilling to pay the price of true sobriety until they have fallen so far that they can't imagine how they got here.

Tim is leading the meeting tonight. He is a pastor and has become one of my closest friends. He gets our attention and then says, "Welcome to this Twelve Step meeting. My name is Tim and I am a recovering addict."

"Hi, Tim." We respond in unison.

"Let's open the meeting with a moment of silence followed by the Serenity Prayer."

After my three months in Miami, I moved back to middle Tennessee. Doris was still living with her sister, so I bought a trashed HUD house to live in. A HUD house is one that has been lost to foreclosure and the government has taken it over. Most of the time it is left empty for so long that, by the time it is purchased at auction, it is nearly uninhabitable. This house had a huge, blue, tarp nailed over the gaping hole in the roof. The back door was hanging on one hinge and the windows were broken out. Animals had lived inside and some of the rooms still held the definite odor and unmistakable stains of doggy doo. (That's a technical building term.)

I bought the house at an auction, moved a cot and a camp stove inside, and started to work. Joshua and Jacob came over every day to help me along, with Josh's best friend, Laban. We gutted the inside, hauling off mounds and mounds of debris, and ripped off most of the roof. When the house was down to a skeleton, we started building it back up. The boys and I worked through the hot summer months. In the early morning we would put shingles on the roof until it got too hot, then we would move inside.

We hung drywall, replaced toilets and laid tile. I took pictures all along the way as the junky, old house came back to life. The boys painted and repainted every square inch of the house. I put new light fixtures in and gas logs in the fireplace. It was a metaphor of our life: this useless, abandoned, old, shell of a structure, after a few months was becoming a gorgeous, warm inviting home.

Towards the end of the summer we had a cookout and world championship croquet tournament at the old farm place where Doris grew up and where her father still lives. I was a little surprised that they invited me to come. Before the family ate, we gathered in a large circle to ask the blessing. I asked Doris's dad if I could say a few words before we prayed. I told them what had happened to me at The Clinic. I told them that I had lied to them before and betrayed their trust in me. I told them about lying to Doris's dad that day before we moved to Miami. I asked them all to accept my apology and begged for forgiveness. The circle fell apart. They fell on me, and hugged me, and cried over me, and welcomed me back into the family. Doris's dad prayed over me and I felt like heaven itself was in that little farmhouse.

In early September, the house was finished and we had a dedication service. Pastor Jeff came and Pastor Jerry, friends from our old church and friends from the new place we worshipped. Our family gathered. All together, there were fifty people, and we went through each room and prayed for God's blessing and protection on that house.

Laban, Josh's friend, had, by now become our adopted son. He had put together a montage of "before and after" pictures of the house, with an inscription that said, "The House of Restoration." He had been Josh's friend since college and watched while I tore our family apart. He spent more than a few late nights playing video games with Josh and Jacob and listening to their heartbroken concerns for me. Laban's parents were divorced and if he didn't know what to say to Josh and Jacob, he at least knew the importance of just being there for them.

We uwrapped Laban's picture. Along with the picture he wrote an essay. We read it and sobbed like babies, all of us. I hung the montage in the family room, over the sofa. It is still one of our prized possessions. Here's the essay:

"One of the most astounding moments of my life was the night I spent with Mrs. Doris, Josh and Jacob, at Mrs. Doris's sister's house. Doris was talking about the brokenness she was enduring and asking us to pray for Pastor Mike. What struck me was how peaceful her spirit was in the midst of that storm. She spoke about the love and strength that she received from the Lord. Her faith was so real and joy poured out of her being. She was able to smile in the middle of the most horrific time anyone could imagine.

A few months later, after God had done a miracle in his life, I was witness to a most humbling experience. Mike had come back, after losing everything. He was sitting in the living room with Josh, Jacob and me and we were discussing our future. He looked around the room and said, 'Well boys,' (I think he likes that phrase.) 'Well boys, it looks like we are all jobless and trying to figure out what we are going to be when we grow up.' I could not imagine the pain Pastor Mike was going through but he made us all laugh and demonstrated a humbleness, an honesty and a sincerity that I have seen in him ever since.

I am certain that God allowed me to participate in the story of your family and see first hand how people, that have come to mean so much to me, have handled being faced with the challenge of brokenness and despair. You have shown me that redemption and restoration is always possible.

This project, fixing up this house, has come to symbolize so much more than the restoration of a house. It has become the restoration of a marriage, of a family, of faith in God. Your story is about joy and peace and true love. It is about God's love and grace and He has used your story to restore me."

The meeting is in full swing. We go around the room and share whatever is on our "top plate," feelings of frustration, fears about the future, stories of victory. We remind each other that we are not alone and that the Twelve Steps and Twelve Traditions keep us focused on a life of honesty, humility and integrity. Each man has heard my story many times and I know most of theirs.

After the dedication service at the house, Doris moved in and life began to get normal. Doris kept her job in Nashville and I began to purchase old houses and fix them up. Jacob enrolled in college. He and Laban moved in with us. Josh stayed in his house, taught school and got serious about Jennifer. After a few months, Doris and I decided to fly back to Miami to attend church there and offer our Step Eight amends to the congregation.

Ashi and his wife met us at the airport and hugged us like long, lost relatives. He prayed for us in the car. He prayed for us in his house. He prayed for us every time we turned around. I have never known a man so free to love and so unwilling to judge as Ashi. He and his wife were the epitome of grace to us.

While we were there, we got word that Jacob was invited to lead the worship on Sunday night at a church near Nashville. We wanted so much to be there. After all that I had put the boys through I felt this was an opportunity for me to thank Jacob and God for standing by me in my mess. We called the airport to change our flight in order to make it back on time. The airline attendant said, "Mr. Courtney, I am sorry but this is one of the busiest weeks of the year. There is no way you can change your flight." Doris and I were sick but Ashi said, "Pastor, let's pray."

The next morning, right after church, we went to the airport anyway, to try and find a flight that would get us back early. Each attendant informed us that the only flight that would get us there on time was overbooked and it was impossible for us to change. I told a young ticket agent, "Son, if you can get us on that flight my wife will kiss you right on the lips." We said we would trust God and wait, but the longer we sat in the terminal, the more difficult it was to believe that God would work a miracle.

Ten minutes after the flight was supposed to leave, the young ticket agent came running up to us, breathless. He grinned and said, "Pucker up, Doris, you're going to Nashville. The flight that was supposed to connect with your flight has been delayed. We have two seats available. It looks like you are going to make it home." Doris and I sat on the front row of a Southwestern jet and wept all the way back to Nashville, thanking God for His amazing faithfulness. (We do a lot of good weeping now.)

We got to the church just as Jacob was taking his band on to the platform. I stood in the back with my hands in the air and my heart in my throat while Jacob sang, "God loves you, and He wants you to know, He is with you. You are not alone. He will see you through, 'cause God loves you." He is such a gifted musician but his talents paled that night beside his obvious abandonment to, and adoration for, the One that had delivered his family and rescued his father from destruction. When the service was over, I sat and watched with pride, and a little awe, as the people flocked around Jacob to express their appreciation for his talent and his heart.

Last Christmas, my sister and brother-in-law gave us an amazing gift. Offered to take us to with them to Israel the next summer. Doris and I said, "No thanks, we'd rather stay home and work in the garden." Yeah, right! What a blessed trip to enjoy the presence of God, walking hand in hand, along the shore of the Sea of Galilee and praying together in the Garden of Gesthemane. Every sacred sight had special meaning for us. At the place where Jesus read in the temple, the tour guide asked me to read. I stood there with my wife and sister and brother-in-law looking on, with the turtle doves cooing in the palms over head and read Isaiah 61:1. "The Spirit of the Sovereign Lord is on me, because He has anointed me to preach good news to the poor. He has sent me to bind up the brokenhearted, to proclaim freedom for the captives and release from darkness for the prisoners." I could hardly read for the tears, thinking that I was the very prisoner that Christ had set free.

Near the end of the trip we toured the Jordan River near the place where Jesus was baptized by John. Our pastor asked if we would like to be baptized and we said, "No, thanks, we'll go home and work in the garden." Yeah, right! Doris and I put on white robes, took off our shoes, and were baptized together in the Jordan River. Someone took a picture of Doris as she came up out of the water. She is simply angelic. There is a supernatural glow about her. I hung that picture on the wall of our family room next to The House of Restoration montage.

While we were there, in Israel, Doris surprised me with a ring, a wedding band. It is hand made by a Jewish craftsmen, white gold, etched with yellow gold. On the band, engraved in Hebrew, is Jeremiah 31:3, "I have loved you with an everlasting love." The double message of that ring is not lost on me and every day when I put it on, I thank God for His love and for my wife.

A week after we came back from Israel, Joshua was married. He was engaged to a beautiful girl that he knew from high school. They had gone their separate ways and now, five years later, God brought them together. Jennifer was teaching high school in Memphis and Josh was teaching outside of Nashville when they started talking again. I am sure she was a comfort to him during my insanity. She loved him, loved his family and even loved me. And we all fell in love with her.

One night during the winter, after the house was finished and life was settling in to a routine, Josh and Jennifer came in and sat on the couch. They shifted and stuttered until we turned off the television and then Josh said, "We are going to get married in July." Why do kids think their parents will be surprised by that? We knew before they did.

Then he said, "Dad, we want you to marry us." I lost it. Two years earlier he did not want to talk to me, he had no faith in me and certainly did not believe I had the right to be a minister. (And he was right.) Now they are asking me to marry them? I was blubbering and sniffling uncontrollably. Doris, always the hero, stepped in. "Josh, I think what your dad is trying to say is that he would be honored to marry you."

They were married on my birthday, in a perfect, outdoor wedding at a picturesque, antebellum plantation house not far from where we live. The weather was ideal. The crowd was huge. The father of the bride paid for everything. It was a perfect day.

They asked for a wedding sermon (that must have been Jennifer's idea), so I spoke on Joshua 1:6-9. "Be strong and courageous for you will lead my people to possess all the land I swore to give their ancestors. Be strong and very courageous. Obey all the laws Moses gave you. Do not turn away from them, and you will be successful in everything you do. Study this Book of the Law continually. Meditate on it day and night so you may be sure to obey all that is in it. Only then will you succeed. I command you--be strong and courageous! Do not be afraid or discouraged. For the Lord your God is with you wherever you go."

I reminded the boys of the promises that God had made to Doris about them, that he would deliver them from the bondage that I had endured and that he had set them free. I told them that the only measure of success was in their faithfulness to God. And I encouraged them to remember that God loves them, here and there and everywhere they would ever go. I reminded Jennifer of the courage that it takes to be a good and godly wife. She turned to look at Doris as I spoke. I promised them that their parents, Jeff and Susan, and Doris and I would faithfully, daily pray for them. And I offered them the blessing of God, the promise of a land that God had already prepared for them if they followed Him. It was one of the great days of my life.

Tim is wrapping up the meeting. I admit I haven't heard much as my mind has wandered over the last two years and the amazing, incredible, spectacular miracles that God has performed in our lives. He gave me an old work truck for free. A few months ago, Doris and I flew to Dallas to appear on James Robison's *Life Today*. We receive phone calls almost weekly from minister families that are battling addictions, infidelities, depression and despair. It is a joyful ministry to be able to work with these couples and pray for their restoration. We tell them that falling is not fatal and failure is not final.

Jacob has been touring with a band all over the Southeast and testifying to what God has done. Joshua is married to an incredible, beautiful Christian girl and they are youth pastors in South Carolina. It has been an unbelievable time.

"It's time for our chips," Tim says. "Here in our fellowship we use a system of chips to denote periods of sobriety. The chips will not keep you sober but they are a symbol of the grace of God and the strength of this fellowship. If you would like to receive a chip please come forward when I call out your period of time." He calls for those wanting a one week chip, a one month chip, a three month chip, a six month chip and a one year chip. No one comes forward. At some meetings several people claim chips and at others, no one.

Tim smiles and looks at me, "Has anybody here been sober for two years?" Everybody in the room is laughing and cheering as I step up to claim my chip. It is a brown, plastic disk, about the size of a half dollar. The back is smooth but on the front is engraved the deep and profound words, "Two Years." Only people who have one know what it is really worth. My guess is the chip cost less than seventy five cents to make. I wouldn't trade it for a million bucks.

Tim hugs me and says congratulations. Everyone in the room is standing and clapping. It is a milestone, not just for me, but for all of us. I did not do this alone. This group was a big part of it, my incredible wife and my loving family, the people at The Clinic and most of all a faithful God. There is a tradition at the meeting when someone gets a chip for more than a year of sobriety. Everyone at the meeting asks, "How did you do it? Tell us the secret of your success."

Success, that's a strange word in a meeting full of addicts. A life of recovery is a life of seeming contradictions. We are healed and helped. We are free when we surrender. We do what is best for ourselves by focusing on others. And we are never really successful until we become complete failures. The only way for an addict to come out on top is by hitting the bottom. My failure is the greatest thing God has ever done for me. It wasn't until I really failed that I learned to be at peace, that I accepted His grace and I knew I was loved. My failure, my very lowest point, was the place where God turned my eyes away from me and pointed me to all He had done for me and all that He would still do. I had to get flat on my back to finally look up and see the future He wanted me to have. The answer just comes to me out of the blue. I grin. "You want to know the secret of my success. When I hit the bottom, I was hoped."

"Therefore I am content with weaknesses, insults, hardships, persecutions, and calamities for the sake of Christ; for whenever I am weak, then I am strong." 2 Corinthians 12:10

SURRENDER, SEX AND SERENITY

One of the most interesting phrases in my stay at The Clinic was the phrase I heard almost daily, sometimes several times a day, from Dr. Carl Rivers. After a particularly poignant story or a dramatic self-realization, Carl would usually ask, "Now, what do you make up about that?" I believe that, implicit in his question, is the concept that every individual has a self-made reality that is partly based on truth and partly based on perception. Two people can go through identical experiences and come away with totally different notions of what really happened that is, of the truth.

It seems to me that the healthy psyche is the one that is able to have an ever increasing percentage of truth, and therefore, an ever decreasing percentage of perception, in his or her reality mix. We will never, this side of heaven, be able to eliminate our own prejudices, preconceived ideas, and self-made belief system from our view of reality. But the goal is to live in such a way that we are able to get closer and closer to seeing the truth. Jesus may have had this in mind when He said in John, "You will know the truth, and the truth will set you free."

The absolute truth of my experience is still not completely clear to me. I am learning everyday to strip way, one layer at a time, a lifetime of false notions and faulty perceptions, and see things as they really are, as God sees them. Having said that, the overwhelming truth in my story is that true serenity comes from total surrender and sexual addiction is more about control than pleasure.

Seven years ago, Joshua and Jacob surprised me with a Christmas present that was totally unexpected. I had always wanted a chocolate Labrador retriever. They are gorgeous, majestic dogs with wonderful dispositions and deep loyalties. On Christmas morning, Josh and Jake came in with the cutest, little, brown puppy you could ever imagine. They had a red bow tied around its neck, which it promptly ate, and my heart was captured. It was not just that this was the dog I had always wanted but also the fact that it came from them. It was their idea and they had purchased this obviously expensive gift with their own money. We named her Coco.

A few months later some suspicions arose about Coco's heritage. Instead of the strong, stocky profile of a young lab, Coco was long and lean. She was skinny. Instead of the rich, deep brown of a chocolate lab, she was turning a rusty red, something like the color of a mud puddle made out of ugly Tennessee red clay. She looked like an embarrassed, eighty pound Chihuahua.

She also failed to exhibit the calm, quiet demeanor of a true lab. Coco was a bundle of nervous energy, uncontrollable in her exuberance and unmeasurable in the brevity of attention span. She ran continually, usually in the direction of away. The slightest opening in the gate of her fenced in back yard was an excuse for Coco to bolt. Calling her generally increased the speed with which she disappeared into traffic, in our busy neighborhood.

I asked Josh one day, "What breeder sold you this defective chocolate lab?" To which he replied, "Well, Dad, it wasn't actually a breeder. It was actually the dog pound. And she isn't actually a chocolate lab. She is really just a mixed-up conglomerate of a lot of different kinds of animals, most of them dogs." Then he added cheerily, "She is kind of brown, though."

Coco was a chewer. She would chew, beyond recognition, anything that she could reach in the back yard. The garden hose, the wires from the phone box, my favorite tennis shoes and the handle of my pitching wedge all fell victim to her sprouting, razor sharp, puppy teeth. One day she even chewed the gas line off of our barbecue grill. The final straw was when I came home with a brand new riding lawnmower. I parked it in the back yard then went inside to change clothes before I mowed with it for the first time. When I came back out, Coco had stuck her head inside the engine and chewed up all of the wires going from ignition to spark plug. It cost one hundred and fifty bucks to fix a lawnmower that I had never used. I was so angry. I went inside and got an electric extension cord, plugged it into the socket on the deck and threw it out across the steps. "Chew that," I challenged Coco. I half expected to see a smoldering clump of smoking, singed fur when I woke up the next day. No such luck.

After about a year of replacing garden hoses and chasing Coco through the neighborhood, I had just about had enough. One night, Coco disappeared. Someone had opened the gate a crack and she was gone. Usually she would return in a few hours, this time she was missing for three days. We drove the streets, put up posters and called the pound. In spite of my frustration over this dumb mutt, I still loved her because of the fact that my sons had bought her for me. I wanted her back.

Late one evening I was walking behind our house and looking and calling. Just on the other side of our fence I heard a whimper. I looked over the fence into the weeds and bushes and there, in a pool of mud and dried blood, laid Coco. Apparently, she had been hit by a car several days ago. She managed to crawl to the back of the yard but couldn't navigate the fence. I could tell by how much the ground around her was scratched bare that she had been there for quite some time, too feeble to move or even bark. She had a compound fracture on her back leg, the skin was torn away in several places on her body and she was barely alive.

I bundled her up and took her to the vet. After a careful examination he told us that she would lose her leg, at best, but probably needed to be humanely euthanized. The amount of care that she would require to have any chance of recovery was more than anyone could be expected to give. As we talked for awhile longer, it became apparent that her situation wasn't hopeless, it would just demand a huge sacrifice. I asked the vet to set her leg and as he worked, we came up with a game plan.

I built a tiny wooden cage in one corner of the garage, complete with a top. It was so small, so confining, that Coco, when she was in it, could not move. This was something the vet said was necessary for her leg to heal. Keeping her in the box meant that I had to hand feed her, give her water from a bottle, and change her bandages several times a day, every day, for many, many weeks. I would set the alarm to wake up in the middle of the night to go out and tend to Coco. As she began to heal I had to manipulate and massage her leg. I would pick her up, this eighty pound Chihuahua, and carry her outside to go to the bathroom, then, carry her back inside.

For nearly three months, Coco was under my complete care and demanded as much of my attention as I could possibly give her. By the end of that time, she was walking, with a pretty severe limp, but walking. She was eating on her own and she was on the way to a complete recovery. In fact, today Coco is a slightly graying, overweight, one hundred pound Chihuahua that greets me every time I come home with an elated wag of the tail, and, if I let her, a kiss on the cheek. And something else, she is completely devoted and totally surrendered to me.

Now I'm no expert on a dog's life, though I think I have lived it a few times, but if you ask me, Coco has it made. She has everything she wants. She is surrounded by people she loves. She has found her true purpose in life, to lay in my parking spot all day and not let anyone else park there until I come home. If there is a doggy heaven, Coco is on her way.

My addiction, like most, was more about being in control of some little piece of my existence than anything else. It became my reality early on that I was out of control. Those people that I loved left me, either by death or divorce. Anyone who really knew me would not like me, and they would leave me too. I was hope-less, helpless and worthless. I had no control of my life, until, I discovered my addiction. Here was one area I could control. I could decide when to get high, and with whom. I could dictate the rules of every illicit relationship. I could keep anyone or everyone from getting too close. Like Coco, I could run away.

Dr. Ralph Earle in his book, <u>Lonely All The Time</u>, describes it this way. "Because their lives are chaotic and unmanageable in general, sex addicts see nearly every aspect of daily living as being controlled by other people. Their employers call the shots at work. Their spouses manipulate and shame them into toeing the line at home. Their parents are able, after all of these years, to stir up feel-ings that addicts see as being out of their control. Everywhere they look, sex addicts see someone else in the driver's seat or someone else's rules and expectations frustrating or confusing them. Sex is the one area in which sex addicts believe they can reclaim some of their power." (<u>Lonely All The Time</u>, pg. 24)

Sounds insane, doesn't it? But in the world that I had constructed, it made perfect sense. The most insane thing, of course, is that the addict is the most out of control person of all but, he or she cannot, or will not, see that. While I don't know as much about other addictions, I have worked with enough alcoholics, drug addicts, eating disorder victims, and addictive personalities, to believe that this is pretty much the case for most addicts. In their addiction, they believe they have control.

If that is the case, then it seems to me that there is a universal truth for addicts. The only way to really be free is to give up control. Surrender is the secret to serenity. It is in giving up what I do not have anyway, that I am able to gain what I do not know I am looking for, peace. Coco's life got good when Coco surren-dered to me.

The proverb that I learned as a child has more to say to me as an addict than almost anything else I have heard or read. Proverbs 3:5-6 says, "Trust in the Lord with all of your heart and lean not on your own understanding. In all of your ways acknowledge Him and He will direct your paths." When I finally began to quit trying to "make it happen" for myself, everything that I longed for was a gift from God. Jesus said, "Seek first the kingdom of God and His righteousness. Then all of your other needs will be met as well." (Matthew 6:33)

The great miracle of hope for me in Scottsdale was not deliverance from some cancer that had me captive. The miracle was that, because I finally saw that God loved me, I was able to surrender the rest of my life to Him. The relationships with my wife, sons, family and friends were all placed in His hands. My future, my job, my finances, all given to Him. How people responded to me, that too is in God's hands. Like Coco in the cage, I have learned to rely on Him for every single aspect of my life, to be surrendered. After all, His Son paid a terrific price for me.

But surrender, I am learning, is a constant battle. There are still probably a few days when Coco looks longingly over the fence, out at the traffic, but a little twinge in her bad hip is all it takes to remember the pain of not being surrendered. Even as I write this book, I can start wondering who will read it, how I should market it, whether or not it will be accepted. All I have to do is feel a little twinge of the still tender scars in my heart and I remember that staying surrendered is the only way for me.

Every morning of every day, before Doris and I leave the house now, we hold hands and pray together. We ask God to protect our sons and our daughter-in-law. We ask His blessing on every church that we have served and on some special pastors in our life. We pray for the list of families that we are working with, asking God to bring them to a place of surrender. Then, we give Him the day. We surrender everything we know and everything we do not know about the day to Him. He is in charge of our finances. He is in charge of our ministry. He is in charge of the bills we can pay and the ones we can't. It's all His.

You know what? That doesn't make us helpless or fearful. It doesn't allow us to be lazy. Remember the Serenity prayer, "God, grant me the serenity to accept the things I cannot change, the courage to change the things I can, and the wisdom to know the difference." We do not surrender and then worry. No, our surrender comes with a secret ingredient. It comes with hope. Every morning of everyday we surrender the day to Him and, every morning of everyday, He is faithful. Now that's a reality I can live with.

A PLAN

Steve Arnette is a good man. He is the pastor of the rapidly growing, incredibly dynamic, First Church in Sioux City. He and his wife Melissa, with their two children, Sarah and Seth, moved there four years ago. It is only the second church they have served but it seems like God has placed them in the perfect position. The people love the Arnettes' and the Arnettes' love the people.

A few months ago, Steve had an affair.

He didn't mean for it to happen. He is in his early-forties, always a good father and faithful husband. He and Melissa married during his freshman year of college and by the time he was a junior, Sarah was born. He worked through college and seminary, was nearly thirty before he took his first church, and it began to feel like life was passing him by. The vulnerability of that, and the pressure of a fast growing church, weakened his resolve and one day, the thing that he never thought could happen, happened.

He is a good man and wants to do what is right, so today, Sunday morning, he is resigning from his church. The affair ended several weeks ago. The guilt and shame of his actions became overwhelming. He wanted desperately to get out but didn't know what to do. He considered running away, disappearing, so that he would not have to face the consequences of his choices, but he loves his family and he is a good man.

Instead, Steve called a couple from Tennessee that he had heard about. They had been through a similar struggle. He did not know why he was calling, only that, in his desperation, he had no where else to go. Within a week of the phone call, Mike and Doris had flown to Sioux City to meet with Steve and Melissa. Together they told Melissa what she already suspected. She and Doris cried together and prayed together, got angry together and just, were together, through the most difficult day of Melissa's life.

After that, they sat down with Sarah and Seth. Sarah is seventeen and just two months away from graduating from high school. Seth is twelve and just got a new baseball glove. Mike and Doris showed them pictures of Josh and Jacob, their own two sons, and talked to them about a beautiful cottage they have access to in the hills of Tennessee. There is a fishing lake, mountain trails, a canoe, video games and a porch swing. Then Steve and Melissa and Sarah and Seth went out for pizza, and Steve told his children what he had done.

After the trip to Sioux City, Mike called the state overseer and explained the situation. He made an appointment for Steve to come in and surrender his minister's license. When Steve went, the state overseer wept and prayed with him, gave him a check for five thousand dollars to help with expenses, and promised his support, and the support of the church. Together they planned the exit for Steve and his family. They met with the church leaders before the end of the week, Steve, Melissa and the state overseer. Steve took two weeks off from the church and the pulpit to get his family on some kind of even keel, and now, this Sunday, he and Melissa will stand together in the pulpit and resign. The church has had time to prepare, the state overseer preached one Sunday and Mike preached the next, and today, the church leaders have planned a beautiful service of thanks and support, as well as a very generous love offering. It will be sad, but it will be a good day. Steve deserves it. He is a good man.

There is no easy or even standard way to handle the incredibly difficult transition that takes place when a pastor falls. There is such a variety of emotions and responses that all involved are staggered by the weight of the situation. The offender is ashamed, afraid, anguished and apologetic. Some times. He or she may, instead, be angry, arrogant, and unwilling to admit his or her sin. The church is saddened, sympathetic and supportive. Some times. Or it may be mad, mean spirited and miserly, instead. Every situation is unique. Every outcome is different.

There are some things, no matter the circumstances, however, that from a biblical and humane perspective ought to be done. There needs to be the possibility of forgiveness and the opportunity for closure. Both church and pastor should have a chance for God's grace to be offered and accepted in a way that will bring healing and even spiritual victory to all concerned. The pastor at his or her worst needs the church at its best. To prevent the encounters that make that possible is to misjudge the power of an incredible God in the very darkest of storms.

For the most part, well meaning denominational church leaders, to protect the church from further damage, have scurried the offending minister out of town and out of the picture as quickly as possible. Fallen clergy are told to resign immediately and have no further contact with the congregation. While the rationale behind this approach is certainly understandable, the sudden separation is devastating for the pastor and family and destructive to the church. Without time to respond gracefully, the church is often splintered by an array of opinions as to what should have been done and the clergy family is deprived of the support that only the people of God can give. Many times, without closure, the minister and family is not allowed the redemptive gift of apology and forgiveness, and the church is wounded more deeply by a secret sin that is unconfessed and unresolved.

All of that is to say, that a better approach may be for denominational leaders to listen with the heart, to each hurting pastor and wounded church and build a plan of restoration and reconciliation as the Spirit of God directs. With an ear more attuned to the love of God than the liability of the church, and with the support of a team of experienced, equipped "restorationists," we may be surprised at how often God is able to be glorified in an otherwise devil delighting event. The lessons we learn by going out of our way to rescue our wounded, rather than shoot them and quickly bury them on the battlefield may revolutionize the church.

My brother-in-law and sister own a small farm in middle-Tennessee complete with a picturesque, two-bedroom, cottage and another cabin as well. We have developed, as you might expect, a relationship with some of the most compassionate and qualified counselors in all of Tennessee, particularly in the area of marriage recovery and, sex and lust addiction. I know of a few churches around Nashville that are as wonderful in their worship as they are open to welcoming the wounded. Their pastoral staff is gifted in welcoming a fallen brother or sister as a peer and making him or her feel like an honored guest. We have access to several affordable rental houses and a network of businessmen that have offered to provide good jobs, jobs with dignity and value, to hurting pastors.

What if, when the word comes to a state overseer's office that a fellow worker has messed up, there was a resource for that overseer to turn to that had a plan in place? What if an evaluation was given to offending clergy, offended family and reeling church, and, based on that, a personalized, and loving, exit strategy was put in place that minimized the damage, maximized the opportunity for grace, and anticipated the wonderful work of God? What if, when appropriate (and many times it would not be) instead of being whisked away and exiled to obscurity, the fallen pastor was given the time, help, and grace necessary to leave with his family less traumatized and his dignity less demolished? What if the hurting church, instead of being isolated from the problem and kept in the dark like an immature infant, was allowed to become the grown-up, body of believers that God desires, and be a part of the healing process? What if......?

There are some, maybe many, situations where such things are not possible. An unrepentant pastor or an angry, vindictive church would make anything less that immediate departure, unwise. The "other party" in an affair must always be considered. The last thing the church wants to do is to cause more harm, or, frankly, invite litigation. But even in these, volatile and painful circumstances, honesty and transparency on the part of all concerned are the only responses that will allow for complete healing. Sin, swept under the carpet, even for the most innocent, will eventually become a stumbling block.

The day after Steve Arnette and his wife left First Church, they flew to Nashville where they were met at the airport by Mike and Doris. After the shock and of the last few weeks, and the emotion of yesterday, neither Steve nor Melissa were capable of making good decisions. It was an amazing relief to have someone step in and take over their lives for a few days. The children, Sarah and Seth, were staying in Sioux City for the next ten days with a wonderful church family that offered to keep them in their schools and with their friends. Steve and Melissa were taken to the "Funny Farm," a retreat center in the woods, where every need was provided for.

For the next two weeks they will drive their loaner car, everyday, twenty miles in to Nashville, where they will meet as individuals, and as a couple, with Dee and Barbi White, two of the most godly and gifted marriage counselors in the area. While in Nashville, they will also meet daily with the pastor of a local church who will be their spiritual guide, praying with them, making reading assignments and evaluating their spiritual needs. Before they leave the city, both Steve and Melissa will attend a daily Twelve Step support group, Steve's group is made up of men who have self destructed because of sexual addictions. Melissa will meet with a group of ladies, spouses of fallen men, who are each day working on their own healing and aiding in the recovery of their husbands.

At the end of two weeks, counselors, spiritual guides, state overseer and Steve and Melissa, will meet in a conference phone call. At that time the recommendations will be made that will help shape the next two years for this family. Perhaps Steve will go to a clinic that specializes in sexual addiction. Many times, an affair by an otherwise good and godly person is a symptom of a much deeper emotional and psychological issue. Such an offender may well benefit from a treatment center. But that may not be the case here, instead, it may be agreed that Steve and Melissa are best served by getting on with their lives and making competent, Christian counseling, a part of their weekly regimen.

In that case, Steve will be offered a job in Nashville and provided with a nice, affordable, rental house. Melissa will go back and stay with the kids, in the parsonage in Sioux City, for two months until school is over. At that point, the whole family will move to a nice home, in an exciting city, with a dynamic church, and a supportive family that, over the next couple of years will assist them all in healing.

During that time, Mike and Doris will go back to the church in Sioux City several times. The church will go through periods of confession, teaching on forgiveness, training in reconciliation, and visioning for the future. When, and if, the time is right, somewhere late in the two year period, Steve and Melissa will come back to Sioux City for a "celebration of healing" service. Steve will publicly testify to his own sin, and to the forgiveness of God. He will make Step Eight restitution to all that He can. Melissa will tell the story of the miracle that God has performed in her family. The church will rejoice in their healing and release them to the future that God has planned for them.

Finally, after two years that have meaning and benefit, not just isolation, Steve and Melissa with be recommissioned for ministry and sent with the denomination's blessing out to battle for the King in way that was never possible before.

- The denomination has prevented the loss of a valuable and gifted asset, a good man.
- Steve and Melissa have saved their marriage and strengthened it with a miracle of healing that has changed them forever.
- Sarah, now a young adult, and Seth, a teenager, have developed a love for, and commitment to, a church that stood by their parents at their darkest moment.
- First Church has become a model to the city and the denomination of grace and forgiveness. Because of

their actions, people from all over Sioux City have been drawn to them and a great revival has broken out.

Mike and Doris, well, they are working with another young couple from upstate New York. And God is smiling to see His children do what they are supposed to do, offer love, acceptance, forgiveness and hope.

RESOURCES

Psychological Counseling Services
7530 E. Angus Drive
Scottsdale. AZ 85251
Tel—480-947-5739
Fax—480-946-7795
pcs@pcsearle.com

Bethesda Workshops
Woodmont Hills Church
3710 Franklin Rd.
Nashville, TN 37204
Tel—866-464-HEAL
info@woodmont.org

Walk With A Limp
Mike and Doris Courtney
827 W. Thompson Lane
Murfreesboro, TN 37129
Tel—615-904-0738
www.mikeanddoris.com

READING LIST

Come Here, Go Away
Dr. Ralph Earle with Susan Meltsner

Lonely All The Time
Dr. Ralph Earle with Dr. Gregory Crow

Pornography Trap: Setting Pastors and Laypersons Free From Sexual Addiction
Ralph Earle, Jr. and Mark Laaser

Out of the Shadows
Patrick Carnes

Breaking Free
Beth Moore

When Godly People Do Ungodly Things
Beth Moore

No Stones
Marnee Ferree

Bibliography

Quotes are taken from the following books and used with permission. They are footnoted throughout the story. My deepest appreciation is offered to the writers and to the publishers.

Alcoholics Anonymous, *"The Big Book,"* Alcoholics Anonymous World Services, Inc, New York City, 2001
Permission to reprint and adapt Twelve Step material does not mean that AA has reviewed or approved the contents of this publication, nor that AA agrees with the views expressed herein. AA is a program of recovery from alcoholism only. Use of material in this publication does not imply otherwise.

Dr. Ralph Earle and Susan Meltsner, *Come Here Go Away*, USA, 1991

Dr. Ralph Earle and Dr. Gregory Crow, *Lonely All The Time*, Tri Star Visual Communications, Phoenix, 1998

Beth Moore, *To Live Is Christ*, Broadman and Holman Publishers, Nashville, 2003

Beth Moore, <u>*Breaking Free*</u>, Broadman and Holman Publishers, Nashville, 2000

Sexaholics Anonymous, *"The White Book,"* SA Literature, Simi Valley, 1989-2002
Permission to reprint and adapt SA material does not mean that SA has reviewed or approved the contents of this publication, nor that SA agrees with the views expressed herein. SA is a program of recovery from sexaholism only. Use of material in this publication does not imply otherwise.